HARLAXTON COLLEGE
UNIVERSITY OF EVANSVILLE
GRANTHAM, LINCS.

THE ANGRY BRIGADE

THE ANGRY BRIGADE

The Cause and the Case

by

GORDON CARR

002634

LONDON
VICTOR GOLLANCZ LTD
1975

ISBN 0 575 01992 1

Printed in Great Britain by
The Camelot Press Ltd, Southampton

CONTENTS

LIST OF ILLUSTRATIONS

ACKNOWLEDGEMENTS

Obviously, in a book of this kind to name some of the most important sources, on both wings of the political divide, would cause nothing but embarrassment. The battle between the Establishment and its opponents shows no sign of diminishing, and if one group knew the extent to which another had co-operated each would, perhaps, be rather less than happy. But I can say that I am indebted to members of the Stoke Newington Eight Defence Committee who provided the transcripts from which the verbatim quotes of the courtroom exchanges are taken. At the same time I am grateful to members of Scotland Yard and the Special Branch for providing their theories and facts so frankly and freely, and in particular to Commander Habershon, who saw Angry Brigade matters more clearly than most. I should also like to thank Brian Michaels and Stuart Christie, who explained some of the political intricacies with patience and tolerance.

As for written material, my main debt is to the dozens of anonymous pamphleteers who have provided so much in the way of "libertarian" literature over the past few years. Two of the "straight" books I leaned on heavily were *Demonstrations and Communications: a case study* by Halloran, Elliot and Murdock, the definitive work on Grosvenor Square, 1968, and, of course, Seale and McConville's *French Revolution*, 1968.

I would like to thank Faber & Faber Ltd for their permission to quote two passages from *Low Intensity Operations* by Frank Kitson.

Much of the information that follows was collected for a BBC TV News Documentary which I wrote and produced in 1973. My thanks, therefore, to Derrick Amoore, the editor of BBC TV News, for allowing me to use it in the book, and to Diana Morton, who did so much of the original research. Finally, my special thanks to Peter Matthews and Bill Norman, the camera team who supported me with patience and discretion through many difficult moments.

G. C.

THE ANGRY BRIGADE

INTRODUCTION

The Carr bombs

THE RIGHT HONOURABLE Robert Carr, Her Majesty's Secretary of State for Employment, had decided to work late. Outside Monkenholt, his large Georgian house in Hadley Green, Hertfordshire, it was cold, damp, not the sort of weather to tempt anyone out unless there was a compelling reason. Inside, Mrs Carr was in the kitchen finishing off the dinner dishes. Thirteen-year-old Virginia Carr had joined her father for coffee in the sitting-room, and before he began work on the papers in his Despatch Box they talked over the day's events.

January 12, 1971, had been particularly difficult for Mr Carr. As the Minister responsible for piloting the Government's controversial Industrial Relations Bill through the Commons he'd been having a rough time, on the floor of the House as well as in the streets outside. Since early that morning thousands of trade unionists had been on the march protesting against the Bill, which they saw as a fundamental threat to their right to protect themselves. Throughout the day there'd been lightning strikes, picketing, clashes with the police, and now late in the evening, at around ten o'clock, a new challenge was about to present itself—a challenge which was to change the whole concept of political subversion in Britain, and a challenge which was to make those responsible for the security of the State take measures which have altered the process of justice itself.

The noise of the explosion brought the Carr family to their feet. A second or so of stunned silence, and then Mr Carr shouted to his wife and daughter to get on to the floor.

"I crawled to the door. Smoke was billowing into the house from outside. I got up and went to the phone, but it wasn't working."

Mr Carr told the family to follow him out of the house and rushed to a neighbour's to dial 999. Then he went back to look at the damage. The kitchen door was missing, completely blown to pieces. Glass and bits of wood were scattered everywhere.

By now a small crowd had gathered across the road from the house, and two police squad cars had arrived. The officers got out and went across to talk to Mr Carr. But before he had had a chance to describe what happened there was another bang, this time at the front of the house, about ten yards away from where they were standing. One of the policemen said:

I saw what I can only describe as a lazy sort of flame three or four feet high coming from the ground near the front door. At first I thought it was a gas pipe burning. But after a few seconds the flame burst into a sheet which rose up the front of Monkenholt as high as the first floor window.

Everybody ran, and then threw themselves to the ground as a second bomb went off with a huge explosion which shattered all the windows at the front of the house and blew in the hall door. As the smoke cleared, and the Carr family made arrangements to stay the night with friends, calls went out to Scotland Yard and to the Home Office with the news that one of Her Majesty's ministers had been attacked by bombs. By chance, that night most of the senior police officers at the Yard were "unobtainable". They had been asked to a special West End showing of the film *Ten Rillington Place*.

The bombs had exploded in S Division, the Metropolitan Police area covering Golders Green, Barnet and West Hendon. In charge of investigations there was Detective Chief Superintendent Roy Habershon, who had taken up duties just a week earlier after a two-year secondment as Assistant Director of Command courses at Bramshill Police College in Hampshire.

In a sense it was almost as if Habershon had been specially trained for the situation that lay ahead of him. He had energy, persistence, but above all he had had several years with the Fraud Squad. Fraud inquiries are unique in criminal investigation in that they allow for "evidence of similar facts". Habershon was therefore used to thinking in terms of "association", and association is, of course, basic to conspiracy. More than most policemen Habershon was trained to look for connections between people and events that were not immediately obvious. But that night as he poked about in the wreckage of

Carr's home he could scarcely have expected that within a week of joining a division noted almost exclusively for the attention burglars give to the large tracts of rich housing within its boundaries, he would be using those qualities at the centre of one of the most complex, bitter and controversial inquiries in police history.

From the beginning Habershon's sense of outrage at the offence was intense.

"It was certainly pretty evident," he said, "that those who were responsible either intended to kill the Carrs, or had such a reckless disregard for them that it amounted to the same thing. I regarded this as attempted murder, and things were set in motion on that basis."

At Barnet police station just after midnight Habershon, Divisional Commander Dace and an explosives expert, Major Victor Henderson, met for a preliminary conference. Major Henderson gave a first opinion on what type of bomb might have caused the explosions and decisions were made on staffing an incident room at Barnet, which would be the headquarters of the hunt for those responsible for the attack.

Habershon himself was quick to appreciate that this was no ordinary case. The political motivation was obvious, and before he went to bed that night he had already resolved to dig out every scrap of information about everyone who had been involved in any sort of political violence in Britain over the previous five years.

It was an area of investigation unique for a detective outside the Special Branch. Habershon knew neither more nor less than any other senior policeman about contemporary British politics. He determined to become a specialist. If he was in any doubt about just how important his inquiries were to become, the following day, on top of the headlines of indignant rage in the papers, there was a statement in the House of Commons by the Home Secretary himself expressing his unreserved condemnation of the crime.

Mr Callaghan, for the Opposition, said, "It is our profound hope that those who have committed this outrage will be brought to justice at the earliest possible moment, and that the country will know that there can be no success attendant on anyone who attempts to influence opinion in any way by means of this sort."

On behalf of the back-bench members, Sir Harry Legge-Bourke, put it this way:

> Everyone inside and outside the House who has a true devotion to the democratic system will be appalled by what has happened, and will wish to congratulate my Right Honourable friend the Secretary of State for Employment on the extraordinary dignity and calm which he has exercised on this occasion. May I express the hope that every possible effort will be made by the Home Secretary and the police to find out who is responsible for this outrage and to expose them for the gross traitors that they are?

So the Angry Brigade, who claimed responsibility for the bomb through communiqués to the press the next day, had finally reached the nation's consciousness. For the first time, people in Britain were being forced into taking the idea of armed revolutionary violence seriously. They had experienced something of the kind before, of course, from the IRA and members of other extremist groups. But while they used the bomb and the gun to achieve specific and highly circumscribed objectives—Home Rule, independence, self-government—those who had attacked Robert Carr's home felt themselves part of a *total* revolutionary process. They wanted finally to change the nature and structure of society itself.

CHAPTER ONE

Political motivation . . . The influence of Debord,
Vaneigem . . . The Strasbourg scandal . . .
Nanterre, the May events

IN HIS STRUGGLE to make some sense of the Carr bomb
attack Habershon had the Special Branch to help him, to point
him in the right direction. He had a lot of questions: just what
kind of person would want to let off a bomb outside the home
of a Cabinet minister? Where were they from? What were their
politics? The Special Branch had very few of the answers.
They did know of the existence of something called the Angry
Brigade through communiqués the group had sent to the
underground press in the previous month. But they had tended
to dismiss them as cranks. Not any more though. The Carr
bombs had made sure of that.

So, again, who were they? Was this the beginning of something really significant: the Revolution, perhaps, that some
people had been predicting for so long? The Angry Brigade
were certainly no part of the traditional trade union movement, despite the timing of their attack on the Employment
Secretary. Nor did they belong to any of the known political
groupings. Special Branch informants came up with nothing.
The answer seemed to lie somewhere in a youthful, vaguely
anarchistic circle so far unfamiliar to the security authorities. But how to identify it? The only slight clue was in an
Angry Brigade communiqué already in the possession of the
police which appeared to be a list of targets: "High Pigs, Judges,
Embassies, Spectacles, Property." It was the word "Spectacles"
that took the eye of one Special Branch Sergeant in particular.
He decided to find out precisely what it meant, and to try to
put it into its social and political context.

Through reading pamphlets, articles and by talking to his
contacts in the anarchist world, the Sergeant soon discovered
that the word "Spectacle" was a concept, emblem almost, of a
group who called themselves Situationists. Two men were
largely responsible for the ideas behind "Situationism"—

Raoul Vaneigem and Guy Debord. They took as a starting-point the belief that the traditional working-class movement started by Marx and Bakunin in the nineteenth century had been defeated over the years, in the East by the Bolsheviks and in the West by the bourgeoisie. Organisations that were supposed to act on behalf of the workers—the trade unions, political parties —had sold out to world capitalism. More than that: capitalism could now take over, "appropriate" even the most radical ideas and "return" them safely against the workers in the shape of harmless ideologies, like socialism or communism.

To remedy all this, in 1957 a group called the Situationist International, mainly artists, architects, intellectuals, set out to develop a new way of looking at, of interpreting, society. It was as part of this process that Debord developed his theory of the Spectacle. He argued that through computers, television, transport and other forms of advanced technology capitalism could control the very conditions of existence. This led to what Debord called the Society of the Spectacle. The world we see is not the real world, it is the world we have been conditioned to see. Life itself has become a show contemplated by an audience and that audience is the proletariat, whom he defined as anyone who had no control over the conditions of his existence. Reality was now something we merely looked at and thought about, not something we experienced.

The net effect of all this, because we have been brainwashed into substituting material things for real experience, was aliena-tion, the separation of person from person. But Debord observed that sometimes the various methods used by the Spectacle to keep people apart—mass culture, commodities, advanced consumer goods—did not work. On the west coast of the United States for example, thousands of young Americans had questioned the roles allotted to them by society. They had run away from middle class, middle morality, middle America and hidden in the anonymous tenements of Haight Ashbury in San Francisco. Another unconscious revolt against the Spectacle, came with the riots in the Los Angeles suburb of Watts in 1965. Thousands of coloured Americans burnt down their own homes and smashed local shops and factories. To Debord these two incidents were evidence of the Spectacle's vulnerability. It could be defeated, but not without real difficulty because it had yet another weapon at its disposal, "Recuperation".

To survive, the Spectacle had to have social control. Recuperation was the way it attained it. Bourgeois society was able to "recuperate" a situation, or resist any challenge to itself, by shifting its ground, by creating new roles and cultural forms. One way of doing this was by encouraging "participation". People were to be allowed a greater say in "the construction of the world of their own alienation". Experimental life-styles were turned into a commodity. Even supposedly rebellious ways of living like the hippies in San Francisco were eventually packaged for cultural consumption. Another method the recuperators used was to deliberately inculcate a nostalgic yearning for the past, keeping people happy by encouraging them to follow the fashions of the twenties, the thirties or the fifties.

But if this sort of measure failed and anyone decided to reject the materialist values offered by the recuperators, then they had a way of coping with that, too. People bored with the mere possession of things were encouraged to possess experiences, through carefully controlled leisure industries and package tours.

The Spectacle not only filled people's time, though, it occupied their environment as well, with something the Situationists defined as "urbanism". That had come about when the recuperators realised that people would no longer accept, and were beginning to resist, the damage the growth of the Spectacle, industry, was doing to their physical surroundings. Haphazard, disordered urban sprawl was replaced by more "manageable" structures—the factory town, the supermarket. Huge tracts of land were developed solely for the purpose of work and profit, with no regard for the real needs of the people forced to live there.

Urbanism also maintained the class system, and class power, by deliberately keeping the workers apart in "little boxes", in isolation. "New architecture, traditionally reserved to satisfy the ruling class, is, for the first time, directly aimed at the poor . . . the mass character of housing leads to formal misery."

The answer to urbanism specifically was the reconstruction of the entire territory according to the needs of the people. The answer to modern society generally was to be nothing less than *The Revolution of Everyday Life*—the title of one of Vaneigem's books.

Unlike most leftist groups, the Situationists were not interested in improving society as it exists at the moment, but in putting something new, and better, in its place:

> To make the world a sensuous extension of man rather than have man remain an instrument of an alien world, is the goal of the Situationist revolution. For us the reconstruction of life and the rebuilding of the world are one and the same desire. To achieve this the tactics of subversion have to be extended from schools, factories, universities, to confront the "Spectacle" directly. Rapid transport systems, shopping centres, museums, as well as the various new forms of culture and the media, must be considered as targets, areas for scandalous activity.

So without political parties, hierarchies of any sort, or the mere transfer of power from one ruling elite to another, the Situationist revolution held out the prospect of the total transformation of the world just when capitalism and communism seemed to have carved it up between them. By taking for themselves a bit of Marxist theory, anarchist practice, by "appropriating" the ideas of modern sociology, and by refusing absolutely to compromise with the ideologies and organisational forms of the old world, the Situationists offered thousands of young people brought up in the affluence of Western societies an attractive cause, and an opportunity to get out and do something about it.

By 1966, with *The Society of the Spectacle* and *The Revolution of Everyday Life* behind them, the Situationists were ready to become a social force. They began to look round for opportunities to "intervene" in existing radical situations, with the idea of speeding up the revolutionary process. The first chance they got was at Strasbourg University late that same year.

Few students in Europe were more apathetic than the seventeen thousand or so at Strasbourg. They were largely middle class, destined for jobs in the professions, science and technology, not much interested in politics, though the student union was controlled by a committee of conventional left wingers.

At the start of the autumn term five Situationists got themselves elected to the union leadership and immediately started to "scandalise" the authorities. They founded a Society for the Rehabilitation of Karl Marx and Ravachol, the nineteenth-century anarchist. They plastered the walls in the streets with a Marxist comic strip, and eventually announced that they were going to dissolve the union itself once and for all. But what angered the city fathers and the university authorities most was their "misuse" of union funds. They spent £500 on the printing and distribution of ten thousand Situationist pamphlets: its full title was: "Of student poverty considered in its economic, political, psychological, sexual, and particularly intellectual aspects, and a modest proposal for its remedy".

The pamphlet, which amounted to a Situationist manifesto, began with a slashing attack on present student attitudes. Students, it claimed, were directly subservient to the two most powerful systems of social control—the family and the State. "He is their well-behaved and grateful child, and like the submissive child he is over eager to please. He celebrates all the values and mystifications of the system, devouring them with all the anxiety of an infant at the breast."

The student's whole life, the pamphlet continued, is beyond his control, and for all he saw of the world he might as well be on another planet:

Every student likes to feel he is a bohemian at heart, but he clings to a false and degraded version of individual revolt. His rent-a-crowd militancy for the latest good cause is an aspect of his real impotence. He does have marginal freedoms, a small area of liberty which has escaped the totalitarian control of the spectacle. His flexible working hours give time for adventure and experiment. But he is a sucker for punishment, and freedom scares him to death. He feels safer in the strait-jacketed space-time of the lecture hall and the weekly essay. He is quite happy with the open prison organised for his benefit. The real poverty of his everyday life finds its immediate compensation in the opium of cultural commodities. He is obliged to discover modern culture as an admiring spectator. He thinks he is avant garde if he's seen the latest Godard or "participated" in the latest happening. He discovers modernity as fast as the market can provide it. For him every rehash of ideas is a cultural revolution. His principal concern is status and he eagerly snaps up all

paperback editions of important and difficult texts which
mass culture has filled the bookstore with. Unfortunately he
can't read, so he devours them with his gaze.

As for the university, it had become a "society for the propaga-
tion of ignorance. High culture has taken on the rhythm of the
production line. Without exception university teachers are
cretins, men who would get the bird from any audience of
schoolboys." There was a time when universities were respected,
but the bygone excellence of bourgeois culture had vanished.
The aim now was a mechanically produced specialist.

The pamphlet pointed out that, away from student life, the
rest of youth had already started to revolt against the boredom
of everyday existence, the dead life that was still the essential
product of modern capitalism. Unconsciously, the new breed of
delinquent, the vandal, the young thug, used violence to
express his rejection of society. He embodied the first side-
effects of urbanism, of the disintegration of values. This kind
of youth despised work, but accepted the goods:

> He wants what the Spectacle offers him, but now, with no
> down payment. In the end the contradiction proves un-
> bearable. Either the lure of the product world proves too
> strong (to this end, to recuperate him, clothes, discs,
> scooters, transistors, purple hearts, all beckon him to the
> land of the consumer) or else he is forced to attack the laws of
> society itself, either by stealing or by moving towards a
> revolutionary conciousness.

The authors dealt with, and scathingly dismissed, existing
student rebels. At Berkeley, for example, on the west coast of
America, the students may have been hostile to current
political structures and policies, but mere hostility was futile,
and would be recuperated. Moreover, abstract opposition to
their own society had led them to sympathise with its apparent
enemies—the bureaucracies of the East, and China in particular, whose cultural revolution was "a pseudo revolt directed
by the most elephantine bureaucracy of modern times".

British dissent also came in for criticism. The revolt of youth
there had first found expression in the peace movement. "The
misty non-violence of the Committee of One Hundred was its

most daring programme." Its finest hour was the Spies for
Peace scandal in 1963. But because it lacked theory the
Committee of One Hundred entered a decline and fell among
the traditional left, or was finally recuperated by the pacifist
conscience.

So what was the answer? The present social system, the
pamphlet suggested, had to be confronted with a worthy
enemy—the negative forces that it produced: "We must destroy
the Spectacle itself, the whole apparatus of the commodity
society. . . . We must abolish the pseudo needs and false desires
which the system manufactures daily in order to preserve its
power."

When the pamphlet was handed out at the official ceremony
to mark the beginning of the Strasbourg academic year, the
outcry was immediate. The press, local, national and international, seized on the incitement to violence.

"From now on," one paper commented, "the international of
young people who are 'against it' is no longer satisfied with
provoking society, but intent on destroying it—on destroying
the very foundations of a society made for the old and the rich
and acceding to a state of freedom without any kind of
restriction whatsoever."

The Rector of the University himself led a chorus of protest.
"These students have insulted their professors. They should be
dealt with by psychiatrists. I don't want to take legal measures
against them. They should be in a lunatic asylum."

Within three weeks the students responsible for printing the
pamphlets were expelled from the university. On 14 December,
the student union was closed by court order. The judge's
summing up was forthright:

> One has only to read what the accused have written for it to
> be obvious that these five students, scarcely more than
> adolescents, lacking all the experience of real life, their minds
> confused by ill-digested philosophical, social and political
> and economic theories, and perplexed by the drab monotony
> of their everyday life, made the empty, arrogant and pathetic
> claim to pass definitive judgements, sinking to outright abuse,
> on their fellow students, their teachers, God, religion and the
> clergy, the government and political systems of the whole
> world. Rejecting all morality these cynics do not hesitate to

condone theft, the destruction of scholarship, the abolition
of work, total subversion and a world wide proletarian
revolution, with unlicensed pleasure as its only goal.

At first the Strasbourg affair did not appear particularly
significant. The furore in the press soon died away, and within
weeks the university was more or less back to normal. But the
longer term influence of the events was enormous. The
attraction of the pamphlet was the attempt in it, perhaps the
first, to provide a set of rules, guidelines, for the bringing on of
a social crisis. The reasoning went like this: everyone knows
that in highly developed countries the forces of revolt exist.
The Committee of One Hundred and the Berkeley rebellion of
1964 were proof of that. But they had collapsed because they
lacked any kind of revolutionary perspective. The people
involved failed to realise that the bomb or free speech were
causes which were the specific signs of a general dissatisfaction
with everyday life. Because of this they had remained specialised
causes, and later became integrated, recuperated or dissolved.
The Strasbourg pamphlet on the other hand provided a new
kind of revolutionary manifesto which offered the theory and
practice of total revolutionary action.

In the months that followed, groups of students at other
universities in France began to adopt the ideas and tactics
of the Situationist International. Their behaviour, the
theatrical nature of their protests, the violence of their
demonstrations, soon led to a nickname. They became known
as *Les Enragés*, after a fanatical eighteenth-century revolutionary
group led by Jacques Roux, who was later guillotined by the
Revolutionary Tribunal. It is not clear who first began to call
these modern revolutionaries *Enragés*, but the word suited their
actions. They were soon "intervening" in the most obvious
provokable situation of the day, the way their own universities
were run.

By the middle of the sixties the French university system was
on the point of total breakdown. The authorities simply could
not cope with the vast overcrowding. At the Sorbonne alone
there were thirty thousand more students than the university
was designed for. To try to deal with the crisis, the Government
founded four completely new universities in the provinces, and
on the outskirts of Paris put up two residential offshoots of the

Sorbonne, one at Orsay, the other at Nanterre, several miles to the west of the city, among the waste disposal tips and sprawling slums of Algerian and Spanish immigrants.

Nothing could be further from the teeming café life, the bookshops and back streets of the Latin Quarter, than the clinically bleak functionalism of Nanterre. It was progressive enough in subjects, with one of the few sociology departments then in France. But there were no common rooms, no cultural facilities, and facing each other like huge council flats across empty tracts of land were the separate residential blocks for men and women.

The sense of isolation at Nanterre was almost complete. Even for the staff, small, detailed administrative decisions, appointments, complaints, were dealt with by a faceless bureaucracy miles away in Paris. The feeling of powerlessness, of non-control, permeated the staff and the students. The kind of alienation that characterised Debord's Spectacular society was at Nanterre for all to see and feel.

To the *Enragés* the situation was almost perfect for "intervention", and the specific ground they chose to fight on was the Department of Sociology, where most of them were studying anyway. They began by helping to draw up a list of reforms. They wanted the right to devise their own methods of work and research, they wanted to revamp the curricula in the light of new knowledge, to specialise in subjects of their own choosing. A committee was formed to work out a formula to submit to the authorities in Paris. But the *Enragés* pressed on with claims they knew would be rejected. All talk of reform was soon lost in the hysteria of ever more militant demands: bourgeois life was oppressive, bourgeois careers were not worth having anyway, it wasn't integration into a corrupt society that students wanted, but the total rejection of it through total opposition.

In support of their claims the *Enragés* disrupted lectures, shouted down the professors. All constructive contact between students and teachers was lost. Rumour spread throughout the campus that plain-clothes police had infiltrated the university to take pictures of the troublemakers. The authorities were thought to be compiling a black-list. Immediately the National Union of French students protested. The "situation" was developing.

In the first three weeks of January, 1968, as the *Enragés* kept up the pressure, the atmosphere at Nanterre was charged with tension. They issued a pamphlet to coincide with the visit to the university of the Minister for Sport, M. François Missoffe, to open a new Olympic-size swimming pool. It announced that there would be "Vandal Orgies" at the poolside at the moment the minister cut the ribbon.

Obscene graffiti were painted on walls and buildings along the official route. At the ceremony itself nothing untoward happened until the end as the minister was leaving. Suddenly, a short, red-haired youth stepped out from the crowd and shouted; "Mr Minister, you've drawn up a report on French youth six hundred pages long but there isn't a word in it about our sexual problems. Why not?" This was a reference to a ministerial document which had just appeared without mentioning the preoccupying student topic of segregated hostels and halls of residence.

"I'm quite willing to discuss the matter with responsible people," the minister replied, "but you are clearly not one of them. I myself prefer sport to sexual education. If you have sexual problems, I suggest you jump into the pool."

"That's what the Hitler Youth used to say." With that famous exchange Daniel Cohn-Bendit, a twenty-three-year-old second-year sociology student, shot into the headlines. But he knew his name had been brought to the notice of the Ministry of the Interior already. Afraid that his visa might not be renewed (though he had been born in France, his parents were German refugees and he had opted for their nationality) he decided to write an apology to Monsieur Missoffe. Officially the matter didn't go any further, but that did not stop rumours that Cohn-Bendit was going to be expelled, and the original issue soon got mixed with suspicion that police informers were active in the university.

The *Enragés* went into action again to exploit the situation. They took some photographs of policemen, blew them up and pasted them on to placards which they paraded up and down the hall of the sociology building in defiance of the university ban on political gestures and demonstrations. One of the administrative staff tried to stop the students carrying their banners. There was a scuffle. The Dean was informed and he decided to call in the police.

It was just what the *Enragés* had been waiting for. Inside an hour four truck-loads of armed police were at the university gates. The Dean signed the papers to let them in, and as they drove through the campus to the sociology building the *Enragés* threw anything they could find at them, taunted them, and ran in front of the trucks to try to draw them into other areas of the campus. As they drew alongside one of the lecture halls the doors were suddenly thrown open, and a thousand students saw with their own eyes evidence of police repression right in their midst.

The police were now no longer a rumour, they were a fact. Moderate students joined in with the rest to force the police back out of the university grounds. It was a classic Situationist victory. Provocation had drawn repression, which in turn had rallied mass support. It gave the *Enragés* heart. They went on disrupting classes, fanning the growing emotional reaction to the authorities. But still they had failed to get any kind of real movement going. That was to come, though, after three bombs had gone off in Paris against American targets as an anti-Vietnam protest. Five young people from the National Committee for Vietnam were arrested. On the evening of 22 March a meeting was arranged at Nanterre ostensibly to protest about the arrests. But after some initial speeches a small group of *Enragés* led some of the demonstrators up one of the tower blocks on the campus to the administrative offices at the top. They burst open the doors, sat down inside, and began to talk. The debate lasted through the night with growing excitement and sense of purpose. Eventually they took a vote on whether it was right to take over the offices and bring politics into the campus. It was carried by one hundred and forty-two to two, with three abstentions.

From those one hundred and forty-two grew the Movement of 22 March and its principal spokesman, or "megaphone" as he preferred to be called, was Daniel Cohn-Bendit. He described himself as "an anarchist by negation". He was opposed to the Marxist-Leninist revolutionary tradition, their dependence on a pyramid structure of command, with the central committee at the top handing the orders downwards to the workers. This form of democratic centralism as it was called was too authoritarian, too hierarchical to provide the kind of political organisation he wanted: that was a horizontal, federal organisation of workers' councils, groups which act together but preserve their autonomy in a kind of direct democracy.

This of course made Cohn-Bendit, and those who thought like him, bitter opponents of the socialist societies of the east.

For me, Soviet society is a form of government which has the characteristics of a class society. In my eyes, bureaucracy represents a class. The Russian working class has no power to make decisions in production and distribution. For this reason, the Soviet State for me is still a class state. I am as opposed to Soviet society as much as I am opposed to capitalist society in France. However, I don't live in Russia, I live here, so I carry on the fight against the French bourgeoisie.

Not everyone in the 22 March Movement shared Cohn-Bendit's views entirely. There were Anarchists, Marxists, Leninists, Trotskyists, and of course Situationists—no one thinker or set of thinkers inspired their activities; they were held together simply by a desire to change society—and that by force if necessary. The movement, as Cohn-Bendit kept on trying to tell a bewildered press, had no organisation, no structure, no hierarchy, no hard and fast programme. He outlined their tactics: There would be no question of over-throwing bourgeois society at one fell swoop. They would stage a series of revolutionary shocks, each one setting off an irreversible process of change. The role of the 22 March Movement was to act as a detonator, without attempting to control the forces it unleashed. Such a revolt couldn't last, but at least it would provide a glimpse of what was possible, of what could happen. He put it this way,

We have developed methods of action, but we have not put forward a theoretical elaboration. If the Nanterre Movement collapses, it will possibly recover in other places with other people. That doesn't matter. It will simply prove that we are incapable of developing this theory. But we are not afraid of that. It'll begin again in another place in another way. It would mean we made mistakes. But this can be found out only in action, in real practice.

At Nanterre, that action and practice had induced what the Dean described as "a real war psychosis". In the end, he decided to close down the Faculty for an unlimited period. The same day, Cohn-Bendit and five of his friends were summoned to appear before a disciplinary hearing of the University of Paris. The charge was not announced, but it was thought to include the harassment of students and insults to staff.

On Friday, 3 May, some five hundred left-wing students gathered in the central courtyard of the Sorbonne to protest about the closure of Nanterre and about the summons against the six students. The Rector of the University, M. Jean Roche, began to worry, particularly as he had heard that a rival group of right-wing students were massing in the streets nearby. He telephoned the Minister for Education, M. Alain Peyrefitte, for advice. The two men decided that the police would have to be called in to clear the courtyard, and the Rector accordingly signed the written authorisation to allow them into the university precincts.

In almost total silence, groups of students were bundled into police trucks parked close to the walls of the university in the Rue de la Sorbonne. As the first load of students, tightly packed on wooden seats behind wire mesh windows, were driven away from the university, a wave of jeering and shouting broke out from the hundreds watching. Suddenly someone threw a stone through the windscreen of one of the trucks. A policeman was cut. The students surged forward, banging the sides of the trucks with their fists. Tear gas was fired. The violence grew and the police lashed out, hitting innocent bystanders as well as the students, who now began to light fires on the roads, tear up paving stones, iron gratings, traffic signs, anything that could be used as a missile. The rioting soon spread to streets far beyond the university, and by the end of the day five hundred and ninety-seven people had been arrested, hundreds more wounded.

The action of the authorities had provided the pent-up anger, resentment and frustration of tens of thousands of young people with a reason for action, and now with an attainable objective. *Libérez nos camarades* was the cry taken up as more and more people joined in. For a week the students held their ground in bigger and more militant street demonstrations until, on Saturday, 11 May, shortly before midnight, M. Pompidou, the Prime Minister, announced that all police would be withdrawn from the Latin Quarter, that the question of the students arrested during the demonstrations would be reconsidered, and that the university would be reopened from Monday, 13 May.

As the news of the rioting and the incredible size of the demonstrations going on in Paris reached the outside world, often through dramatic TV news film of the fires, barricades, and the violence, thousands of young people from all over Europe began to flock in, not only the leaders of companion groups in other countries, but also individual men and women, drawn by something they felt was relevant to their own situation. Among those who went there from Britain were several from Cambridge University, including John Barker, who was reading English at Clare College. Barker spoke French fluently, and was soon involving himself in the activities at the Sorbonne in particular. He, and Anna Mendelson from Essex University, and Christopher Bott from Strathclyde, were just three among hundreds of intelligent, politically conscious young who were profoundly affected by the Paris experience. "A good time to be free," was how Bott put it. "In the slogan of the time 'Imagination was seizing power'."

As soon as the CRS moved out of the Sorbonne, the students moved in, at first in small groups, then in hundreds, later in thousands. The place was suddenly transformed from a fusty precinct for the training of technocrats and bureaucrats of the French administrative system into a revolutionary volcano. Everything was suddenly up for discussion, for question, for challenge. Day and night every lecture theatre was packed out, the scene of continuous and passionate debate on every subject. One English student there caught the spirit of those early days in a pamphlet he wrote for the Solidarity group.

The first impression was of a gigantic lid suddenly lifted, of pent-up thoughts and aspirations suddenly exploding, on being released from the realm of dreams into the realm of the real and the possible. In changing their environment people themselves were changed. Those who had never dared say anything suddenly felt their thoughts to be the most important thing in the world—and said so. The shy became communicative. The helpless and isolated suddenly discovered that collective power lay in their hands. The traditionally apathetic suddenly realised the intensity of their involvement. A tremendous surge of community and cohesion gripped those who had previously seen themselves as isolated and impotent puppets, dominated by institutions that they could neither control nor understand. People just went up and talked to one another without a trace of self-consciousness. This state of euphoria lasted throughout the whole fortnight I was there.

At the Sorbonne there was a proliferation of posters and wall slogans, much of it Situationist inspired. In the passageways, corridors, hundreds of people stopped to read "The tears of the Philistine are the nectar of the gods", "Go and die in Naples, with the *Club Méditerranée*", "Long live communication, down with telecommunication". Near the main entrance was a big sign, *Défense d'interdire*—"Forbidding is Forbidden". Others variously expressed the theme "We will refuse the roles assigned to us".

But while the Sorbonne got all the attention, all the glamour, all the argument and debate, in a kind of student soviet, not far away, at the Centre Censier, an enormous ultra modern building built as the new faculty of letters, the Situationist International and the *Enragés* were forming, with others, the Council for the Maintenance of the Occupations.

They wanted to set up worker-student action committees to take advantage of the series of strikes and sit-ins that were spreading from Paris to the rest of France. By Tuesday, 21 May, ten million French workers were on strike. In most factories there were occupations, discussions about management, and arguments about the future of society in general. The nation's transport system was totally paralysed, though essential services were kept going. From professional footballers to art gallery owners people supported the movement, but like everyone else they were waiting for the next step. They had taken over the factories, formed their own action committees, thrown open the doors of the institutions—but now what?

The tiny group of students at the Censier tried to tell them how to follow it all up. They began to turn out leaflets with the theme of self-management, rank and file control, and the idea of workers' councils. The people at the Censier also denounced the "recuperators", those who wanted to direct the Paris events towards reforms, or towards their own party ends—because that was what was already happening.

The French Communist party, which was alarmed by a situation if had not foreseen and could not control, began to fight back. Their paper, *L'Humanité*, bitterly attacked the 22 March Movement and Cohn-Bendit himself: "Such false revolutionaries must be energetically unmasked, because objectively they serve the interests of Gaullist power and of the great capitalist monopolies."

Cohn-Bendit for his part referred to the Communist party as "the Stalinist filth". The giant CGT, the principal Communist trade union in France, with its system of cells under the control of a rigid central committee, allowed no dissent. They wanted no truck with insurrection of the kind demanded by the students. They wanted revolution, but within the legality of the republic, and carefully controlled by the politburo of the French Communist party. Eventually, the CGT dissociated itself from the students altogether.

Meantime, the French government, mystified and alarmed by its loss of control, searched round for a solution. The official opposition had called for elections to solve the crisis, with a transitional government made up of orthodox socialists. But the Communist party would not have that, so nothing was done.

At last de Gaulle decided to act. On 28 May he made a secret flight to Baden Baden in West Germany to consult with the commander of French troops stationed there, General Massu. He wanted to make sure that the army was still loyal and would back the legal government in any possible confrontation.

With an assurance from General Massu that they would support him, de Gaulle returned to Paris the following day, and prepared his ground. He called in the prime minister, M. Pompidou, and the whole of the cabinet and told them that he was going to dissolve the National Assembly and call for a fresh election as soon as it was practicable. Then at 4:30 in the afternoon, he spoke to the nation. The country, he said, was threatened by a Communist dictatorship, but the Republic would not abdicate. Everyone must act to help the government in Paris. The Prefects in the provinces would be given wide powers, and the President hinted that if the troubles continued, he would not hesitate to use "other means", no doubt a reference to General Massu's troops.

The words *vive la France* had scarcely died away from the

Graffiti sprayed on the wall of the Old Bailey during the Angry Brigade/Stoke Newington Eight trial in 1972

DEAR BOSS

YOU HAVE BEEN SENTENCED
TO DEATH BY THE REVOLUTIONARY
TRIBUNAL FOR CRIMES OF OPPRESSION
AGAINST MANY WHO ARE OPPOSED TO
THE CAPITALIST REGEIME WHICH YOU
KEEP IN POWER.

THE EXECUTIONER HAS BEEN SEVERLY
REPRIMANDED FOR FAILING. HE WILL
MAKE NO FURTHER MISTAKES.

BUTCH CASSIDY

THE SUNDANCE KID P.P.THE TRIBUNAL

You can dream up all
the law & order you like.
But remember, you are
subject to OUR justice.

HE WHO LIVETH OFF
THE PEOPLE —
BY THE PEOPLE
SHALL HE DIE

The Wild Bunch

Above: Facsimile of a letter sent to Sir John Waldron after the bomb at his Roehampton home

Right: Facsimile of a letter sent to Sir Peter Rawlinson, who was then Attorney General, after the bomb attack on his London home

millions of television sets and radios throughout the country
before the first Gaullist supporters were on the streets,
organising massive demonstrations of loyalty. The fear of
communism and a desire to hit back brought the centre and
the right flooding to the Place de la Concorde, for a huge and
carefully planned march down the Champs Elysées to the
Eternal Flame at the Arc de Triomphe—the symbol of national-
ism and patriotism. The silent majority, helped by extra petrol
rations and coaches to drive them in from all over France, put on
a display of solidarity and strength that outmatched anything
the unions, or the left, had been able to muster.

At the elections that followed, de Gaulle was returned with
the biggest parliamentary majority he or anyone else had had
in recent French history.

The reasons for the ease with which the French revolution
was "recuperated" by the Establishment have been analysed
in depth over the years. It was always true that despite the
millions of people on strike, and the hundreds of thousands who
demonstrated on the streets, the movement was the work of an
intellectual elite. They had managed to bring out in French
society discontent with the increasing distance between the
order-givers and the order-takers, between the bureaucrats and
those whose lives they seemed to control, between the workers
who were told to expect rewards and a state which could not
provide them.

Despite the sit-ins and factory occupations, the vast majority
of people still wanted to pursue the material comforts and
benefits to be got from society as it existed at the time. They
could not understand, and were intolerant of, the cultural
suffocation felt by the intellectuals. For the workers, Debord
and Vaneigem, the Spectacular Society, *The Revolution of
Everyday Life*, were all so much idle rubbish when set against the
"realities" of their struggle for economic survival. And anyway
the concepts themselves were so difficult as to be practically
meaningless.

Nevertheless, the revolution was a close-run thing. It took all
de Gaulle's political experience and strength of will to prevent
the country falling apart. Slowly his government recovered the
state property taken over by the revolutionaries, the flags were
taken down, the slogans painted over. Hundreds of foreign
students drawn to France to take part in the events were

deported, including Cohn-Bendit and John Barker. They went back to their respective homes, profoundly affected by the days and nights on the barricades, by the exhilaration of new ideas. Surely, they felt, advanced capitalist society could never be the same again. Revolution had been shown to be possible, and made possible, some believed, by the theories and above all by the practice of the Situationist International. The idea of "intervening" in a situation through the deliberate and systematic provocation of the kind used by the 22 March Movement had worked dramatically. Each of their pinpricks had succeeded in escalating the conflict the way they wished. They had proved that with the right kind of detonator the explosion could be massive.

As for the traditional revolutionary groups, they had hardly come out of it all with much credit. The French Communist party was instrumental in getting the strikers back to work. It was offered power, but it did not take it, basically because it was no longer in its nature to be revolutionary. To the young, it appeared to mouth class slogans without believing in them any more. It was mesmerised by the pursuit of affluence, of cars and television sets; the communists were obviously slaves of the Spectacular society.

There was criticism too of the other left groups, who seemed to be incapable of ridding themselves of their old routines and ideas, incapable of learning or of forgetting anything, dissipating their energies in quarrelling among themselves.

They failed to understand, or at least if they did, gave little attention to, the new type of issues that emerged during the disturbances, particularly the idea of self-management (autogestion), which seemed to many to be the key to the whole episode. The traditional left despised, or simply ridiculed, the anti-hierarchic, anarchist notions of the hard core 22 March Movement. But it was precisely those ideas that had given the May events their impetus in the first place. Under the influence of the revolutionary students, thousands of people began to question the whole principle of hierarchy. They had shown that democratic self-management was possible, and had begun to practise it themselves through the action committees and the factory occupations. No matter how bizarre, even absurd, the ideas expressed by Debord and Vaneigem might seem, no matter how puerile the Strasbourg pamphlet might read, thousands of young people recognised in them their own kind of radicalism, a radicalism which was no longer reflected by the traditional political groupings. The "ideology gap" began to fill with a kind of revolutionary libertarianism which Barker, Mendelson and other veterans of the Paris experience brought back to Britain in the summer of 1968. It took some kind of hold at most universities, but stuck fastest at two in particular—oddly parallel to the Sorbonne and Nanterre—at Cambridge and Essex.

CHAPTER TWO

*Essex, Cambridge . . . The "disappointments" of
Grosvenor Square, October 1968 . . . The campaign
against Assessment*

ESSEX UNIVERSITY, LIKE Nanterre, was plonked on a
piece of land in the early sixties to ease the growing demand for
places. It, too, was built in tower blocks like a council estate
with little sense of style. Many of the students were from
working-class backgrounds, first generation undergraduates.
And if there was not much in the way of social tradition, there
was even less academic tradition, with new subjects, courses, and
a heavy emphasis on sociology. Intellectually, socially and
geographically, then, the students were isolated. They did not
have to read Debord to learn what alienation was about. It was
an experience close to them all, and perhaps that was one
reason at least why Essex of all British universities was such a
fertile ground for protest. The sit-ins, demonstrations and
strikes were almost a tradition in themselves.

Into this disruptive and somewhat disillusioning atmosphere,
at the start of the autumn term of 1967, came two attractive
and intelligent young girls fresh from schools where nothing
very much in the way of politics or controversy of any sort had
ever taken hold. Anna Mendelson, from the local girls' High
school in Stockport, where her father was a Labour Alderman,
enrolled for a course in English literature and American
history. Hilary Creek, from a private school in Bristol, started a
course in History. Within weeks both girls were drawn to the
groups organised to protest against anything, from the way the
university was run, to the current political issues of Vietnam
and Cambodia. At Essex it did not take long for those
predisposed to rebel to find a cause and sympathetic support.

Essex University's alienation from the mainstream of British
academic life may have been responsible for this sense of defiant
resentment, but it was equally possible to feel anger at the most
traditional of the country's educational institutions. In 1967
John Barker, one of the brighter sixth-formers at Haberdashers'

Aske's, won a scholarship to Clare College, Cambridge. He went up that autumn to live in digs at 7 Regent's Terrace. His landlord was a local policeman. At Trinity, a few streets away, in the same college as Prince Charles, Jim Greenfield was starting a course in medicine, backed by five "A" levels.

Barker was a Londoner. His father was a journalist. Greenfield came from the North, from Widnes. He described it as "a small, dirty, working-class town where the rate of bronchitis was the highest in the country". His father was a long-distance lorry driver. Greenfield has explained graphically and succinctly the effect Cambridge had on him:

> The place I grew up in is an area of high unemployment. And pretty well everyone I knew was trying hard to get out. Working hard, getting to university, was my particular way out. But when I got there it was like suddenly being thrown into a completely different world where all the attitudes I knew as a kid were back to front. I would be meeting people whose attitudes appeared to be really viciously anti-working class.
>
> First of all I put it down to the fact I was meeting a few individuals who were particularly unpleasant people. But eventually as I spent longer in the place it became obvious it was down to the fact that people you were meeting every day were the sons and daughters of the British ruling class, and they have the same nasty prejudicial attitudes as the ruling class has had for generations. I made a decision for myself at that time, that whatever I was going to do with the rest of my life, it certainly was not going to involve helping or aiding or abetting those people or their class to get any more rich or powerful than they were.

In his first few months at Cambridge Greefield decided that reading medicine was a mistake. The course took up a lot of time, and even by Cambridge standards the people on it with him were conservative, antagonistic. The economics department was a good deal more progressive, and the subject politically useful. He decided to ask for, and was granted, permission to change.

Barker was equally disenchanted with his first taste of Cambridge, though in his case not so much because he saw it as a social affront. He was concerned rather with the university's intellectual limitations. He had read, understood, and later translated some of the works of Debord and Vaneigem, and that, combined with his experiences in Paris, gave him a certain prestige among revolutionary inclined students. Those who had actually been involved in the May events could quote from first hand knowledge and they regularly tried to pass on the spell to their less politicised fellows, who had merely read about it all in the papers, or seen it on television.

As part of an attempt to get through to "an apathetic, stultified student body" as he called them Barker and a group of friends, Greenfield among them, "got into radical theatre". The plays they put on, sometimes outside on street corners, at the market, anywhere they could attract an audience, were simple explicit attacks on the issues of the day. One particularly startling performance was an enactment of the suffering caused by American bombing of North Vietnam. Whether, of course, the sight of half a dozen young people, their faces painted white and wearing homemade Chinese hats, shouting and wailing outside the local supermarket did more than irritate the passers-by is open to question. But it did give a great deal of self-confidence to the people taking part.

On a more sophisticated level, in an attempt to emulate the notoriety of the Strasbourg pamphlet, Cambridge had its broadsheet, which Barker helped to distribute. The exact authorship was not disclosed, but the authorities saw it as emanating from the Kim Philby Dining Club, founded by a group of Cambridge Situationists in honour of the man they regarded as having done more than any other in recent times to undermine and embarrass the Establishment.

The broadsheet borrowed many of the ideas expressed in the Strasbourg pamphlet and applied them to the situation at Cambridge. From its very foundation, the argument went, the university was a landowning institution. Architecturally, even, Cambridge expressed the ideology of the landowning class. Entering a college was like entering a French château, and just as a landowner had to be protected from the surrounding peasantry, so it was no accident that since the academics moved into Cambridge, the local people had been ruthlessly uprooted and moved out. It followed, therefore, that unless the student chose to identify with the Establishment, he was oppressed rather than uplifted by the beauty of his surroundings because they represented what he had been deprived of—"the expropriation of his cultural history by a ruling elite".

Barker, Greenfield and the handful of students who felt as they did, saw the university as "a cultural appendage of ruling class violence and exploitation". It was not right, they felt, that the university should be able to keep industry out of the town in order to depress the wages of those who maintained its aristocratic lifestyle. It was not right that libraries and rooms should lie idle, forbidden to local students and townspeople. It was not right that the university should own acres of unproductive land in the centre of the town, while the townfolk were forced out on to council estate wildernesses, that it should own street after street of empty houses while rents soared and the homeless were abandoned.

The broadsheet argued that a university should devote itself to human liberation rather than to its containment and repression. Its educational structure should be based on participation rather than hierarchy. Status and authority would come from "the spontaneous respect for knowledge and intellect and action". At this "critical" university, students would work on the strategy and tactics of social change and revolution, as opposed to the present preoccupation with counter-insurgency, social pacification and control. The "critical" university would commit itself to helping the revolutionary struggle everywhere, and in this way it would overcome the greatest fault of all in the present system—the separation of theory and practice.

The idea that theory and practice, thought and action, are one and the same goes a long way to explain the life that Barker, Greenfield and many others like them began to follow. They argued that only by clearly acting on one's principles could one remain an honest and integrated person, only by actively taking part in social progress and social struggles could one gain a valid understanding of society. No one could be revolutionised by introspection, by reading books and studying political theories. One had to organise a programme for oneself of action and confrontation. For the young revolutionaries at Cambridge, and everywhere else in Europe for that matter, 27 October, 1968, was to provide an opportunity to try out those ideas, to try once again to create a situation "beyond the point of no return". Paris had failed, would Grosvenor Square, perhaps, fulfil that revolutionary promise?

On Saturday, 15 June, 1968, at a conference held at the London School of Economics, a national organisation of socialist students declared itself in being with the title The Revolutionary Socialist Students Federation. Their manifesto contained, among other things, commitment to all "anti-imperialist, anti-capitalist struggles, to the revolutionary overthrow of capitalism and imperialism, and its replacement with workers' power". Its aims, it said, could not be achieved through parliamentary means, and therefore it considered itself as an extra-parliamentary opposition. Whether by accident or design is not clear, but the RSSF conference coincided with a visit to London of many of the student leaders who had been active in Paris, including Daniel Cohn-Bendit. They had been invited to take part in a BBC programme on recent developments in the student movement, and their presence, and the climate of increasing student militancy, opened up the possibility to those who were looking for it that the huge anti-Vietnam war demonstration organised for 27 October just might be the start of something on the lines of the Paris rebellion.

If anyone doubted that the whole meaning of public demonstrations was changing, they had only to read the October issue of the CND paper, *Sanity*:

> This is a new type of demonstration. It stems from an increasing recognition that violence is inherent in Western Capitalist societies. Violence is proclaimed by a situation where power is unequally distributed and decisions are made by a minority "up there". . . . There is violence in the alienation of the worker from his own work.

The last sentence could have been written by Debord himself. As a reason for taking part in the demonstration, this was a long way from CND, Vietnam Solidarity, Committee of One Hundred, or any of the traditional protest movements. The ultimate revolutionary aim was put clearly in *Black Dwarf*, the underground paper edited by Tariq Ali, one of the principal organisers of the march.

27 October should not be seen as an end in itself but as the beginning of a new movement. All left wing groups should get together and set up a joint co-ordinating committee to be called the Extra-Parliamentary Opposition. Such a party cannot be built in isolation from the mass of those who are active on the streets against the Vietnam war, because they are the politicised vanguard and will of necessity form the cadres of a new party.

But, as Tariq Ali told a press conference a few days before the demonstration, "We don't want any mindless militancy. We don't want any confrontations with the police." He was against the arguments publicised by Herbert Marcuse, the American social philosopher, that demonstrators should actively seek confrontations by attacking the police, ". . . the visible symbols of the repressive nature of the capitalist system". In that context confrontation with the police symbolised the struggle of oppressed peoples everywhere to liberate themselves. Grosvenor Square was simply to be regarded as a symbolic Vietnam. That was one argument for violence on the march, but there was another, of course, the one used by the veterans of Nanterre. In its crudest form their aim was to provoke the authorities into repressive action. That repression, as an example of the iniquities of the state, could then be used to gain sympathy and support. But that depended, of course, on getting the "right" kind of response from the police. Would they react to provocation like the CRS in Paris or the police in the Chicago student riots earlier that summer? Certainly the press and television companies were expecting violence. In London there had been several clashes between police and demonstrators over the preceding twelve months. John Barker himself was arrested at the particularly violent demonstration in October, 1967. He was already an old hand: "When I was fourteen or so I went on demonstrations—Ban the Bomb—and learned the role of the filth (pigs, Old Bill, what you like) and to mistrust. . . . I was pissed off with people getting nicked at all the demos, simply caused by people not being together."

So just how would the police tackle what promised to be the biggest demonstration of protest ever held in Britain? Some changes were obviously needed, and indeed they were made. At Scotland Yard new tactics were evolved. First of all the

Yard agreed to allow the march to proceed along its staged route and not to interfere unless there was violence to persons or attempts to damage property. Then they decided they would allow the marchers the whole width of the road, and that they would not try to divide them up or even split the column to allow traffic to cross. All roads leading on to the route were closed. Police reinforcements in buses were parked discreetly out of sight in side streets. Mounted police in particular were stationed so that they could see the route, but the marchers could not see them until they were up to them. Other measures were simple, even obvious. The police were now told how to deploy themselves properly. They were taught to link arms. They went into the demonstration with more discipline than ever before. The logistics were also improved. Mobile canteen facilities were provided, and meal breaks were staggered so that individual policemen, who had probably given up a free week-end anyway, did not have to queue for hours, growing more irritable. It all helped to make the police better humoured when eventually they came face to face with the demonstrators. Nothing was more calculated to make a young constable lose his temper and break ranks to "have a go" at a marcher than being cooped up in a stuffy coach for hours without food, and on a day perhaps when he would have been out with his girlfriend.

As for the march organisers, Tariq Ali had already made it plain he did not want confrontation, and as the column wound its way through the London streets he constantly warned about discipline through a loud-hailer. His aim, and the aim of the vast majority of the marchers, was to proceed peacefully through the streets to a final rally in Hyde Park. But, as in previous marches, a breakaway group were determined that the objective should be the American Embassy in Grosvenor Square itself. That was obviously where the confrontation they were looking for would take place. They accused Tariq Ali and his organisers, especially the Vietnam Solidarity Committee, of diverting the march away from the main target, the American Embassy. They urged by leaflet and loud-hailer "all marchers to unite in a single demonstration and march to the US Embassy, the lair of the aggressors".

Just after four o'clock the police in Grosvenor Square could hear the breakaway group approaching. Chief Superintendent Deats, from his position on horseback behind the cordon, guarding the front of the Embassy, shouted his final instructions through his megaphone. "Our job is to maintain the police line in accordance with your instructions. There will be no incidents." The breakaway group, carrying a variety of banners, Britain-Vietnam Solidarity Front, Action Committee for Anti-Imperialist Solidarity, and several anarchist flags, entered the square and came to a halt about fifty yards from the police cordon. After several minutes of chanting and shouting they began to press forward, about twenty or so actually trying to push the cordon directly, with another hundred pushing from behind. The technique used by the police to deal with these attempts to break through their lines was to give way at the point of pressure, crowding in at the demonstrators from the side, trying as it were to pinch them off from the main group. On one occasion a group of about fifty demonstrators drew back from the cordon for about five yards and then with their heads down charged at the cordon. The police receiving the brunt of the impact gave ground while again those at the sides pushed inwards. It forced the demonstrators into an arrowhead formation and robbed them of their momentum. The police line held firm. Eventually at about eight o'clock, as it was beginning to get dark, the police moved out against the crowd, thinning now, that remained in the square. They moved very slowly, giving people plenty of time to get back. As the square was cleared there were no incidents, and the Home Secretary, Mr Callaghan, publicly congratulated the police on the way they had handled a potentially explosive situation. As if to add a final touch, a group of demonstrators joined the police left in Grosvenor Square in a rendering of Auld Lang Syne. It was an act that drew nothing but contempt from those who had been hoping for some real clash with authority, some explosive outcome. It confirmed how the Establishment had simply managed to recuperate the situation. As a "situation" in the Situationist sense, the whole Grosvenor Square episode had obviously been a complete failure. The notion that the security forces could be provoked in Britain, as they had been in France earlier in the year, proved false.

For the new revolutionaries, demonstrations of the Grosvenor Square kind had become "institutionalised". More than that, they were being used by the state to prepare, organise, and try out its own defensive systems. They were used for "counterinsurgence manœuvres". John Barker said the whole thing seemed to have gone backwards since the Committee of One Hundred days, and he now dismissed Grosvenor Square as a "hypnotic, genital urge—a trap". By the end of 1968, to redeem the revolutionary promise of the start of the year, other methods had to be found.

Back at Cambridge, Barker, Greenfield and their group, because of the Grosvenor Square fiasco, were now even more convinced of the need for more direct forms of attack on the Establishment. They embarked on a campaign against that part of it nearest to hand—the university. Theoretically, the idea was to "sharpen and crystallise the social contradictions at the university and in British society as a whole". In practice it took the form of the kind of behaviour the Situationists had used at Nanterre and other universities on the continent. Stretching over several months there were sit-ins, forced debates, occupations, disruptions of lectures, graffiti on the college walls, but perhaps the most melodramatic gestures came with the so-called campaign against Assessment.

At its simplest the campaign was a protest against the existing system of examinations and degrees as a way of judging someone, of deciding into which slot in society he or she should be put. Clearly, they reasoned, examinations fulfilled little or no academic function, they did not teach anyone anything. They were designed to force the student to study what the government, industry and the media wanted. They saw them simply as a formal device for instilling into the student the bourgeois ideology which made up the contents of the course. Academics were "intellectual whores" who consistently placed themselves at the disposal of the ruling class either as consultants or as apologists for the system. Leaning heavily on the Strasbourg pamphlet, the argument went on: "Examinations induce a sense of passivity in the student in the face of authority and tradition. They encourage him to fit in. They also stultify his critical awareness of himself, of what he's supposed to be doing at university, and of the society in which he's placed."

Barker, Greenfield and others who took part in the campaign against Assessment, felt they were being brainwashed by Cambridge. They saw their lives as students as a constant battle for personal survival. Their identities were threatened by the traditions, the rules, the "external categorisations" they felt the university was imposing on them. Creative and fulfilling relationships were distorted, they felt, by their forced involvement in a system of competition and "institutionalised morality".

Trying to put across these ideas in an almost totally hostile environment was the first real experience Barker and Greenfield had of what might be called a political campaign. It was a taste of what they would be up against later. They learned about the practical side of protest politics, about meetings, committees, how to get people to listen, how to produce leaflets and pamphlets. Barker, for example, also learnt how to produce silkscreen posters.

In June, 1969, in a last and consistent gesture against the university, its role in society, and their personal rejection of it, Barker and several of his friends ripped up their final exam papers and went down from Cambridge for good. With that melodramatic gesture behind them their aim now, as freshly committed revolutionaries, was to ally themselves with other oppressed and subversive forces in society, and in their struggle for personal liberation, work for the liberation of society as a whole.

CHAPTER THREE

Notting Hill . . . The squatting movement . . . The Claimants Union and "real" politics

BARKER AND GREENFIELD came down from Cambridge to London not knowing quite what to do next. Barker went to stay at his parents' house in Willesden and a few days later Greenfield joined him, largely to see what London was like. He had not really spent much time there in the past. First they got a job on a building site at Berkhamsted, but it folded after a couple of weeks, so to earn some money they decided to set up a stall in Queen's Crescent market in Camden, selling second-hand books. As Barker put it: "We made enough money to live, selling books at weekends. And although we had to work during the week trying to get more stock, it did give us quite a lot of free time to get to know more people in London, and especially people who shared basically our desire to live in a socialist society."

One place he met like-minded people was at the poster workshop in Camden High Road. He had heard they were producing posters in support of the GLC rent strike. "They needed some help, and because I'd done poster work at Cambridge I went over there to help." It was there that Barker met Christopher Bott for the first time. Bott, after his experiences in Paris, was now interesting himself in the Solidarity group, who follow ideas propounded by the French revolutionary socialist, Paul Cardan. But though Barker and Greenfield were attracted by some of the ideas of Solidarity, self-management and workers' councils in particular, it lacked the total revolutionary commitment they were looking for, and found at the beginning of 1970 in Notting Hill Gate.

Powis Square, London, W.11, stripped of its former elegance to a Rachmanite slum, was living evidence of capitalist society in decay. Even the gardens round which the large, once opulent, terraced houses were originally built had been concreted over and enclosed by a high wire netting fence so that it looked like a prison compound. In dilapidated rooms anonymous families crowded together, always afraid of eviction from what seemed the last chance of cheap unfurnished accommodation. Here, clearly visible, was the kind of "oppression" revolutionaries wrote and talked about. If ever Barker, Greenfield and dozens of others who felt as they did, needed confirmation of their beliefs, Notting Hill was their witness.

Barker moved into 25 Powis Square with a young Greek, Mike Sirros, who had reputedly fought with the Canadian separatist group, the FLQ, and who had gained entry to Britain illegally. Soon Barker was joining in the underground life of the community, playing an ever-increasing part. Round the corner from Powis Square was the Notting Hill Peoples' Association with its meeting rooms and coffee bar at 90 Talbot Road. At number 89 lived another group of community activists—among them Jerry Osner, Sarah Poulikakou, and Chris Allen. Barker joined them in the Notting Hill Carnival, helping to build floats and organise the events.

On another occasion Barker heard that Kensington and Chelsea council were going to sell off two houses they owned to private speculators:

> We had information that a deal had been worked out between the speculators and nobody was going to bid above a certain figure. A lot of people were annoyed that in a Borough where there were so many people without houses at all the Council should be selling them off to speculators. So a group of us went down to this auction held in Chelsea Town Hall, dolled up in the best clothes we had. It was just like a normal auction and the bidding went up to about £20,000. It was at that figure that we thought they had agreed to stop, so then we started bidding. There were about six or seven of us sitting round the room, and the bidding went up and up. Some of the speculators actually took it seriously and started bidding against us. I don't think it was until we got to about £75,000 for one house that the auctioneer suddenly realised what was happening, and of course, there was pandemonium.

But Barker and his friends in Notting Hill were also involving themselves in more serious political activity. Many of the workers in the district were employed by the giant GEC-AEI factory at Harlesden. The firm had recently merged under the control of Arnold Weinstock, and statements put out by the management talked about the "rationalisation" of jobs as a result. With some of the men from the factory and some of his friends from Cambridge, Barker produced a leaflet explaining that "rationalisation" was merely a polite way of saying "redundancy", and that the merger would benefit only those who ran the company or who had shares in it. Barker went round to all the company's London factories handing out the leaflet to workers as they left for home.

This was the sort of thing that Greenfield decided he wanted to do as well, so he set about looking for a permanent place to live in London.

It was a difficult and depressing business. He concentrated his search on the notice boards of London University. One day, as Greenfield was scanning the advertisements at the London School of Economics, in a hall nearby a meeting in protest about the American invasion of Cambodia was just breaking up. One of the girls coming out of the hall caught his attention. He followed her and eventually got into a conversation and went for a coffee. The girl was Anna Mendelson.

"We got on really well together," said Greenfield. Anna herself was living in another depressed area of London, in York Way, just behind King's Cross. She introduced Greenfield to her friends, at that time mostly contemporaries from Essex University and mostly living a semi-communal life at 168 Stamford Hill. Among the girls there was Hilary Creek, like Anna Mendelson, now down from Essex without a degree, and devoting her time to community politics.

The arguments for living communally were both practical and political. On the practical side the benefits were obvious enough. Sharing food, clothes, books, rent, cleaning, cut down on expenditure, and boring chores, and with the right kind of "affinity" there was a reassuring protectiveness, a solidarity against outsiders, particularly authority. For some people commune life offered the kind of security they had lacked in the family they had been brought up in. Others found in the commune a substitute for the family they had never had.

On a political level, another reason for the communal way of life was to help put into practice one of the basic tenets and more difficult demands of the "libertarian" revolution—the abolition of the family unit as the fundamental part of the social fabric of society. The family unit, the argument went, was an authoritarian unit, with power exercised by the father over his children and over his wife. Wilhelm Reich was the main theorist here. According to him, sexual repression was the way parents gained control of their children, and it was also the way the state gained control of the people who lived in it. Therefore getting rid of sexual repression meant freeing oneself of state control. In this process of sexual liberation the commune was a useful, if not an essential, ingredient, as it was for forming people in general to fit the society that would evolve once the libertarian revolution was over.

In several areas of North London young men and women were trying out these experiments in lifestyle. They varied in their degree of politicisation. One particular commune in Grosvenor Avenue, where several of Barker's Cambridge friends had based themselves, was involved specifically in revolutionary anarchism and the women's liberation movement. One room was set aside for research and writing on the life and death of the Italian anarchist, Giuseppe Pinelli—a name already synonymous with state oppression in the minds of many young revolutionaries.

A letter home by one person who lived at Grosvenor Avenue for a while describes some of the problems the birth of a baby had on the commune:

Since the intention of the people there is to live collectively, and not in isolation from each other, they looked on the occasion as one of sharing the mother's burden and taking collective responsibility in looking after and bringing up the kid. There are eight rooms, kitchen and bathroom. Four women live there and five men, but the number fluctuates. All the women are involved in the women's liberation movement. The baby's arrival was a time for the practical application of ideals, of alternative ways of living. The mother from the beginning did not want to breast-feed the baby so that it did not build a dependence on her, and come to see her as being the centre of the universe. The baby, in fact, was looked after by different people all the time. In practice, it means that someone stays the night with her and during the day. There are charts of feeds, changes, steriliser unit changes, so that things do not get overdone.

Obviously not all such "communes" were as politicised as Grosvenor Avenue. Many were made up of people interested jointly in "single issues"—Gay Liberation, prisoners' aid, drug rehabilitation, women's liberation. Whatever the specialised interest in a particular commune, the people involved moved out into the world to practise it, sure of a secure base behind them. The group Jim Greenfield had been introduced to by Anna Mendelson at 168 Stamford Hill was heavily involved in the squatting movement.

In November, 1968, when a group of libertarian activists decided to apply direct action techniques to the problem of homelessness, they started with careful legal and local research. They established that if certain obvious precautions were taken, if for example they did not force entry to a squat, then there was nothing illegal about taking over empty property. Again, once they had barred themselves in, it took a civil court order to get them out. On occasions, when the authorities discovered that no legal process could get rid of the squatters, they resorted to direct action themselves—either through forcible eviction by the police or sometimes by hiring gangs of self-styled bailiffs, to break down the barricades and force their way in. Anna Mendelson told Greenfield about the work she and her friends were doing among the squatters in Hackney. In particular she told him about a block of empty flats in Arbour Square next door to Stepney police station. Some thirty families were squatting there in defiance of the Tower Hamlets council, who owned the premises. Greenfield, she said, should see what it was like for himself. He did.

The plight of homeless families in the depressed areas of London made a particularly strong impression on people like Barker, Greenfield, Creek and Mendelson. After all, they, too, had experienced at Essex and Cambridge a similar sense of dispossession, out of placeness, alienation. They were genuinely shocked by the conditions they came up against. Greenfield described Duncan House in Hackney, the council reception centre for the homeless, as "a falling down, rat infested old slum". It was known officially as Part III accommodation—accommodation provided by the local councils for emergency housing. But they felt it was simply a place where the council put people they refused to house, when, in fact, all around them in Hackney and Dalston there were perfectly respectable flats and houses lying empty just because the councils refused to rent them out.

But Greenfield and his libertarian friends saw more in the Squatting movement than an obvious remedy for homelessness. They recognised at once its revolutionary potential. It gave people a little more control over their own lives. It was a real exercise in self-management. By taking over empty property and by organising it for themselves on their own terms, people as a group took away a small amount of power from the authorities. It also provided a measure of community control, and perhaps above all as far as the Situationist-inspired revolutionaries were concerned, squatting provided the opportunity for a direct confrontation with the authorities.

This was reason enough to attract Greenfield to the squatting movement in general, and because of his connections with Stamford Hill, to Arbour Square in particular. Within weeks of meeting Anna Mendelson, he had thrown himself wholeheartedly into the work of helping the squatters and their families, often working twelve to fifteen hours a day. He soon got a reputation in the area as a handyman, someone who could plaster, do a bit of carpentry or plumbing.

For the people who took part, this activity among the squats was a social and political education, the practice to go with the theory. First of all they had to spend time learning about masses of legal formalities like writs of eviction, the law of trespass, the Rent Act, they had to learn how local government worked. They also had to protect themselves and their accommodation physically from evicting bailiffs, the police, and from landlords. They had to defend themselves from other people in the street who were not squatting, and who objected, often violently, to their presence. Greenfield and two of his friends formed a special squad to look after squats. They made sure they were there when the law arrived, they looked into the legal aspect of it all. Their lives were a continual fight, often physical, with authority. In Hackney for example, they demanded meetings with local councillors, invaded the council chamber during debates on housing, shouting and throwing leaflets about.

Not everyone involved in helping with the Arbour Square squat was happy about the way the revolutionaries were steering their confrontation course. Some wanted to negotiate with the council to try to get a better deal for the families, but this was denounced as a reformist sell out. Bitter rows broke out among the militants themselves, the families became demoralised and began to leave. The revolutionary potential of Arbour Square was becoming exhausted. It was time to look elsewhere, to move on.

In January, 1970, the bookstall Barker and Greenfield had been running in Queen's Crescent market was scarcely supporting them. So Barker decided to look for work at his local Labour Exchange. But he found that the people behind the counter were highly suspicious of a young man with so many educational qualifications apparently willing, even anxious, to accept any kind of menial job. He felt they marked him out from the start as a trouble-maker, a militant, an organiser. In the end he gave up trying to get a job and decided to apply for unemployment benefit. In that simple act, Barker found for the first time since he had left Cambridge confirmation of the kind of oppression he had set his mind to fight. If Greenfield at that time saw the best prospects for the libertarian revolution coming through the squatting movement, Barker was to see the revolutionary potential of the process of claiming social benefit.

He had never before had to tackle the complex business of filling in forms to get what he felt was rightfully his:

There was always this incredible aggravation with the officials at the offices. People weren't getting what was due to them because, he said, "they couldn't understand the forms, or didn't know their rights, didn't know what they could claim". The whole process of claiming social security seemed to him like one great obstacle race. The attitude was "Come back tomorrow", and tomorrow it was "Come back on Thursday". No one got anything without three or four trips. As he and his friends saw it, the Department of Health and Social Security was an old hand at dodging demands, with a tradition going back to the Elizabethan Poor Laws. The hours spent shuffling back and forwards, or sitting round in stuffy, uncomfortable offices, were meant to drive home the system's underlying premise that "the only way you are allowed to support yourself is by sweating it out on a production line".

There was also a feeling that the people behind the counters seemed to regard the money they handled as though it was their own. They doled it out with a grudge, as a favour. Supplementary benefit in particular had to be bargained for. Because of their isolation and the fact that they were kept in ignorance of their legitimate rights, most claimants were really scared of the whole business of collecting social security, of confronting officials. One answer to all this was obviously for people with claims on social security to get together, to help each other. Barker discovered that a group in Birmingham were already forming themselves into something of this sort. They called themselves a Claimants Union, taking the word "claimant" from the definition used in the 1966 Social Security Act.

"Because of the situation I was in myself, it made a lot of sense to me," he said, and set out to find out more about it. Perhaps the most distinctive feature of the Claimants Union and what made it attractive to people like Barker was the fact that they believed in total control of the union by all members in it. Everyone had an equal say in decision making. There was no hierarchy, no leadership. They took pains to make sure that older members, office holders, experts, indispensable activists were never allowed to dictate policy. The essence of it as an organisation was control by the rank and file. Specifically, the role of the Claimants Union was to ensure that everyone in it, and all members had to be on social security, got what was due to him, whether he was deserving or undeserving. They tried to follow each individual claim through to a successful conclusion. The tactics were clearly laid down:

Go to your local social security office as regularly as possible. Don't be fobbed off by the *Receptionist*. He or she should not make a decision on your claim, but only take your name and address. Don't be fobbed off by verbal indecision, excuses, references, codes, acts, etc. Most times it is just bluff. Always go to the office as a group. Always go into the interviewing cubicles in pairs or threes. Always take leaflets with you when you go. Never leave the cubicle until you are satisfied. Don't let them keep you waiting all day long. Ring the Regional Office and complain, or better still, get everyone in the office to fill in a Complaint form.

Don't just back up other claimants. Get them to back you up as well. This is the best way of getting across the idea of mutual support. It will encourage the claimant to feel part of the union's work, encourage him to join. Getting to know as many claimants as possible is vital, for it is at the social security office that the C.U.'s most important day to day work is done, and where your potential mass strength lies.

Amassing solidarity among the outer fringes of society, then, was really what the Claimants Union was about. The people involved were the unemployed, willing or unwilling, the sick, the aged, the single parent, strikers, anyone with an income low enough to qualify for free school meals, rent or rate rebates, family income supplement, as well as those in the Claimants Union who saw these disadvantaged members of society as the base of a vast revolutionary army. There would be tenants fighting against the means test associated with the Housing Finance Act, squatters fighting against property speculators, prisoners, brown or black people, gay men and women fighting repression and prejudice. These small, local, democratically controlled groups, highly flexible in approach and tactics, could succeed against the Establishment where traditional top-heavy and rigid bureaucracies had failed.

We want power to destroy the means-test system and the values attached to it, such as the work ethic, which we deplore. Nobody is going to offer us this power. We have to take it and run our own lives. And when we demand a say in our own lives we do not mean participation. What we mean is Claimants' self-management of the Welfare state, and a guaranteed income for all people without a means test.

So went Claimants' manifesto, based on the view that the Welfare State itself was a con.

Social security is for the security of the state. A modern advanced technology cannot operate with an undernourished and semi-literate working class. "Our movement (Claimants Union) must challenge the whole nature and purpose of 'work' in this society. We musn't batter on the doors of the present system for re-admittance to the treadmill of wage slavery. *Wages* are the expression of the price of labour as a commodity, like nuts and bolts, and not as real living human beings. We want an adequate income for all without condition. A welfare system should feed, clothe, and provide for *all* its citizens *as of right*. The present system fails to do this. Every Claimant's daily existence is a maddening struggle against poverty, under-nourishment, depression, boredom, despondency and anxiety. We want more than just a rise in the benefit scales. We demand a minimum income per person (every single member of the population) with no strings attached."

Naturally, only a tiny majority of Claimants subscribed to that kind of philosophy. Most imagined the Claimants Union as some kind of super social work organisation designed to help them with their problems. People who had been used to regarding themselves as problem cases, and who liked having things done *for* them, on their behalf, by the State, were often shocked by the fact that they had to put into it as much as everyone else. But the Claimants Union gave them some kind of collective experience, often for the first time. For Barker, on the other hand, and those who felt like him, the appeal of the Claimants Union was the anti-authoritarian nature of the structure and the ideas behind it. "Self management in practice" was how he described it. With Pauline Conroy and one or two other people living in Notting Hill, Barker formed the West London Claimants Union. About ten to fifteen people attended the first meeting. But it soon grew, and so did the frequent confrontations with social security officials, sometimes ending in physical violence.

All this communal activity was happening at a period in their lives when Greenfield, Barker and their friends were most politically receptive. As the experience of the conditions they met up with broadened, and as their clashes with authority increased, they started to see the wider implications of the situation they were in. The sense of alienation they felt from their university days, superimposed on the conditions they found themselves living in, hardened their attitudes into a desire for an all out attack on society itself. Barker got from the Claimants Union, for example, "the great experience of learning to resist, as comrades, as a community". He said that taking part in the build-up of the movement was the most important thing he had ever done.

This was "real politics"; the politics you make yourself. What you do with other people who are in the same position as you. The task of building an effective group, whether it was a squat, a claimants' union, a women's liberation workshop, a tenants' association, the task of countering and negotiating with the authorities, was much more demanding than the occasional weekend demonstration that often passed for political involvement. It was a long way from the traditional form of left wing revolutionary activity—groups who looked over their shoulders to 1917, to the kind of revolution that took place in Russia, the kind of revolution that would take place in Britain after some cataclysmic event—a general strike, or economic breakdown, a *coup d'état*. To the new libertarian, the revolution was now a continuing and growing process. They dismissed the International Socialists, the International Marxist Group, the Workers' Revolutionary Party, all the Trotskyist groups, as far too authoritarian, more concerned with building political parties than in developing political consciousness. These elitists, as they were called, believe the workers do not and cannot understand what society is all about, so they will lead them, they will bring the light to the masses. But to Barker and Greenfield this "apartness" was much the same kind of thing they had been fighting against in the squats and through the Claimants Union against welfare officers and social workers who did things *for* people on behalf of the state. It was substituting one kind of political oppression for another. And it was oppression above all they were against. Not only, of course, in political life, but in social and sexual life, too, which is why, of course, they gave support to, and began to organise round, groups like the Gay Liberation Front, and the women's movement in general.

What Barker, Greenfield, Mendelson, Creek and the growing band of revolutionary libertarians were determined to do was to help all "oppressed" minorities to resist authority, and to resist authority with them. Organised into self-managed groups they provided a militant political force firmly based in the community. They were in the front line of resistance and in conflict with local authority, the police and the state itself. But so far this resistance meant physical confrontation with authority from a "legal" individual position. There was no question at present of any kind of armed "resistance". Nor was there any kind of co-ordination of the activities going on in libertarian circles. People were working in many different areas of community life. Often they were unaware of what was going on in districts separated by just a few miles. But there was, in Britain, a revolutionary group with a different background who had been engaged in acts of violence—bombing and machine gunning—from as far back as 1967. For anyone wanting to take the fight against society a stage further into general urban guerrilla activity, there was an example on hand with experience, expertise and contacts formed over a generation.

CHAPTER FOUR

The influence of the First of May Group . . . The decision to bomb . . . The deal . . . The joint campaign begins

ONE EVENING LATE in February, 1970, Barker, Greenfield and some of their friends gathered at the offices of Freedom Press in Whitechapel High Street to attend a meeting arranged by the International Black Cross, a long-standing anarchist prisoners' aid organisation revived by Stuart Christie, a young Scotsman who had spent three and a half years in Spanish gaols for smuggling explosives. The principal guest of the evening was Miguel Garcia, a Spanish anarchist from the Civil War period now living in Britain after serving twenty years inside. Christie, who had met Garcia while they were both in Carabanchel prison, did most of the talking. Garcia had lost his voice. The shock of his release had led to paralysis in some of the muscles in his throat. But his revolutionary spirit was undiminished. Through Christie, as the story of his adventures and deprivations at the hands of the Spanish authorities unfolded, he made it plain that he was as determined as ever to carry on the struggle.

For the fifty or so in the audience, most of them young people for whom the Spanish Civil War was firmly in the history books, it was an emotional occasion. In front of them, in person, was someone who had been in direct confrontation with the state, who had been totally involved in resistance struggles, and who had paid a heavy penalty. He, and Christie for that matter, were examples of revolutionary working class anarchism in action. Both had anarchist contacts all over the world, in particular through the Iberian Federation of Libertarian Youth—the FIJL—founded in 1932 as the youth sector of the Spanish anarchist trade union organisation, the CNT, now for the most part exiled in Toulouse.

The FIJL, through the Spanish Civil War and the Second World War, had accumulated a vast experience of guerrilla fighting. To counter penetration and infiltration by Franco's secret police, they evolved their famous affinity groups, *Grupos de Afinidad*, which later became the model for the modern urban guerrilla group. In fact the FIJL can lay claim to producing the first truly *revolutionary* urban guerrilla cell.

The First of May Group emerged from the Spanish movement as an international, anti-capitalist, anti-imperialist revolutionary organisation, specially structured to carry out terrorist attacks. It took its name from its first operation carried out on 1 May, 1966. The ecclesiastic adviser to the Spanish Embassy at the Vatican, Monsignor Marcos Ussia, was kidnapped on his way home to his house in the suburbs of Rome. For days, Italian, French and Spanish police searched for him without success. Then, after he had been missing for about a fortnight, he was released with a statement saying that the action had been undertaken to draw attention to the plight of political prisoners in Spanish gaols. It was signed: "The First of May Group".

But soon the group was taking in a much broader area of attack, and even, in case there should be any misunderstanding, produced a spokesman. "*El Largo*", "*Gros Jean*", or properly, Octavio Alberola, had led a dashing, not to say romantic, life since his father settled in Mexico at the end of the Second World War to escape from Franco's secret police.

With Raoul and Fidel Castro and Che Guevara, Alberola helped to found the Latin American Anti-Dictatorial Front, the power base from which eventually they were to topple the Batista regime in Cuba. He was also active in the FIJL, and consequently he soon ran into trouble with the Mexican authorities, who regarded him as a dangerous agitator. He was arrested for spreading political propaganda, and after a month in prison released on the orders of President Corines, but only on condition that he took no further part in any kind of political activity. It was asking too much of a man like Alberola, so in 1957, with a false name and passport, he slipped out of the country and returned to Europe to live a clandestine life among anarchists, inside and outside Spain.

Exactly how Alberola came to be involved with the First of May Group is very much in dispute. The security services of Britain, France and Belgium are convinced that he was a founder member and took part in many of their actions. He himself says that these are charges put about by the Spanish secret police. He was simply the group's public relations man, its essential link with the outside world. To back this up he cites a "pres: conference" he gave in 1967 in the United States.

Rumours in newspapers at the time suggested that the First of May Group was out to kidnap the American Ambassador to Spain, Mr Biddle Duke. To set the record straight, Alberola went to New York himself to explain "Operation Durruti", as the plot was to be called.

At a supposedly secret press conference in the Manhattan Hotel, Alberola said that the real target was to have been the Commander in Chief of the American forces in Spain, Rear Admiral Norman Gillette. The idea was to take him to Madrid, and to make him listen, in front of reporters, to a denunciation of America's presence in Spain.

Alberola warned at the press conference that although "Operation Durruti" had failed, the First of May activities would go on, inside and outside Spain. He was not exaggerating. In the twelve months that followed, from the middle of 1967 to the summer of 1968, there were dozens of bomb explosions and machine gun attacks all over Europe. Britain had more than its share.

On the night of 20 August, 1967, at exactly a quarter past eleven, a white Ford Cortina drove down Park Lane in the West End. In the car were three First of May men. They turned into Grosvenor Square, drew alongside the American Embassy, and without slowing down fired a burst from a 1938 Beretta sub-machine gun into the plate glass frontage. As the car sped away into the West End, they threw out a leaflet. It read "Stop criminal murders of the American Army. Solidarity with all people battling against Yankee fascism all over the world. Racism no. Freedom for American Negroes. Revolutionary Solidarity Movement."

The following day, the remains of the bullets and the spent cartridge cases were sent to the Metropolitan Police forensic science laboratory in Richbell Place, Holborn, for microscopic examination. At the same time a letter was posted to Reuters news agency from Hounslow explaining the reasons for the attack more fully:

1. As the Johnson and Macnamara murderers are continuing their "escalade" against people fighting for their freedom,

another "escalade", that of the Revolutionary Solidarity Movement, is now beginning in the whole world against Yankee fascism.

2. We are on the side of all Latin American *Guerilleros* and American Negroes fighting against racist and economic oppression of Yankee capitalism.

3. American people must know the danger of their own government's criminal fascist politics which is the main supporter of all dictatorships in the world.

The letter was signed "Revolutionary Solidarity Movement. First of May Group".

This use of a "communiqué" to explain the reasons for a particular act of violence began with the First of May Group. They were also the first to use "concerted" attacks. Six months after the Grosvenor Square shooting, on 3 March, 1968, six bombs went off within minutes of each other in six locations in three European cities. Property was damaged in Turin, The Hague and in London, where explosions shook the Spanish Embassy in Belgrave Square and the American Officers Club in Lancaster Gate. No one was injured, but as an exercise in co-ordinated violence, it was impressive.

The next First of May attack in Britain came in February, 1969. The targets were Spanish-owned banks: two in London, one in Liverpool. The two London bombs failed to explode and were taken to the explosives laboratory at Woolwich for examination.

The communiqué issued at the time was addressed to "the Pentagon and White House killers". It proclaimed that "every man who doesn't want to go down on his knees to you can only reply by revolutionary direct action to your world terrorist planning".

Just over a month later, a bomb went off outside the Bank of Bilbao in King Street, Covent Garden. But quite by chance two policemen were sitting in a car on routine patrol some thirty yards away. They watched as two men strolled up to the bank entrance and placed a parcel in the doorway. Suddenly smoke billowed out into the street, the men began to run, the police got out of the car and raced after them. When they caught and searched them, they found another First of May communiqué in one of their pockets:

Sirs, the imprisonments, deportations, and murders suffered by the people of Spain since their subjection in the Civil War, the garrotted, and those who died by the hand of Francisco Franco oblige us to respond. The blood of our brothers is as precious to us as the money and the property belonging to Spanish capitalists and their Wall Street colleagues. Let them hear this week another noise other than the clink of bloodied silver. Cease the repression. If not expect more widespread reprisals. The International 1st of May Group.

At Freedom Press that February night in 1969, the significance, the importance of the First of May Group, and the tradition it sprang from, was not lost on the people crammed into the tiny room to listen to Garcia and Christie. It was not so much what they had to say that impressed them (anti-Franco activity was specific, nationalistic, and a long way from the squats and social security offices of Notting Hill), it was the stand they had taken, and of course the fact that they had actually "done time for the cause".

By their activities in the Claimants Union and the Squatting movement, Barker, Greenfield and others in the audience had already rejected the classical forms of protest. The kind of direct action they were getting involved in, contained in the end the philosophy of the urban guerrilla. Here in front of them were two men who had carried direct action into that ultimate area.

It need not necessarily have been the Spanish movement which influenced those looking for action, it could have been any other urban guerrilla group. By 1969–70 there were plenty around, largely developed as an answer to the disappointments of 1968. In the United States, for example, the Weathermen urban guerrillas had set out to attack the capitalist system with a wave of bombing on banks, company offices, schools and military installations. The Baader-Meinhoff group was getting under way in West Germany. There were revolutionary urban guerrilla cells in Turkey, Italy, Japan, Switzerland and Holland as well. And in Britain, the new libertarian consciousness that had been developing in the latter half of the sixties was to be given a sense of direction by a tradition of urban guerrilla activity stretching back a generation.

Exactly what was going through the minds of Barker,

Greenfield and the others as they walked down Whitechapel High Street on their way back to their flats in Notting Hill and North London, no one can tell. But around that time, certainly within weeks of the meeting, they had made a decision to follow the First of May's example and start some sort of armed resistance against the state. The reasons are obviously complex, and not everyone involved shared the same ones. Some were drawn to the idea out of the simple frustration and anger they felt about the conditions they saw in the squats and squalor of the London slums. For others, it was an almost inevitable escalation from the kind of direct action they had been involved in since the campaign against Assessment, the Squatting movement and the Claimants Unions, to what they thought of as a higher, more developed level of resistance in terms of organised, armed violence. Again, others were plainly conscious of the failures of 1968. The revolutionary techniques used in Paris and later in Grosvenor Square had got them nowhere. They could see no alternative to bombing as a facet of class struggle, but bombing in conjunction with propaganda, communiqués, newspaper articles. To these people, physical violence was a defensive action against what they felt was the increasing hegemony of the state: "hitting back", as some of the graffiti of the time had it. Then there were the arguments about the nature of violence itself, arguments outlined in the works of Debord and Vaneigem. The violence inherent in the Spectacular society. The violence of the production line, of the high-rise flat, state violence perpetrated on people in their everyday lives. To attack those responsible for this gave them a taste of the violence they were responsible for in the first place. It may have been somewhat abstruse, but it was strongly felt by those involved.

The ruling class just defines violence in terms of a violent picket, or a violent crime or a violent bank robbery, or a violent bomb going off, which totally distorts the real essence of what violence is. What violence is, is the fact that people end up in a situation where they are so freaked about the way they live, that they beat up the people they love. What people wanted to do was to try to show that that level of violence should be channelled towards the people who are actually creating the situation of oppression in the first place.

In other words, a group of people were going to take this new definition of violence, pirated from the Situationists, and try to show that it was possible to channel it "into a much more constructive direction". Another explanation for the decision to bomb went like this:

> It's a message passed on to the ruling class. Okay, your conspiracy will continue, and the bombs won't make that much difference to the way it operates. But it's going to be just a little bit more difficult for you. We're not just going to sit around and produce petitions against what you're doing. The bombings are not going to be the be-all and end-all of the situation. They're an announcement of a certain situation where we're no longer going to accept the confines of legality set by the state.

Those last few words: "no longer accept the confines of legality set by the state" were the real warning, the decisive step from protest within the law to violence outside it. But so far they were just words. First, there were some practical considerations. Would, for example, the First of May Group, who were essential for the supply of gelignite, expertise, and weapons, have anything to do with these unknown, though obviously enthusiastic, libertarians? Down the network to Paris and Brussels went the suggestion, back to London came the reply. A limited amount of help would be given in the way of weapons and explosives in exchange for one or two reliable people to help with the concerted First of May campaign going on throughout Europe at that time.

It seemed a reasonable deal. What the First of May got out of it, aside from a new bombing team, was a strengthened libertarian resistance movement in Britain. What the new libertarians got out of it of course was access to urban guerrilla experience, ammunition, explosives and guns. The targets the new group would go for would reflect traditional First of May interests and much broader libertarian solidarity with social and political situations in the country at large.

So after a gap of almost fifteen months following the arrest of the two Bank of Bilbao bombers, the First of May Group was ready to strike in Britain again. This time the target was Iberia Airlines at airports in four European cities. In London a man

The home in Hadley Green of the Secretary for Employment, Mr Robert Carr, showing damage to the house and car the morning after two bombs exploded on 12 January, 1971

359 Amhurst Road: the house in Stoke Newington where Barker, Creek, Mendelson and Greenfield were living when police raided on 20 August, 1971

COMMUNIQUE ₁0
THE ANGRY
BRIGADE

Pictures released by Scotland Yard of weapons and gelignite found
in the top flat at 359 Amhurst Road together with the Angry
Brigade stamp

telephoned Scotland Yard to say that a bomb had been put on board an Iberia Airline plane at Heathrow. The passengers were taken off and told to claim their luggage. Sure enough, the last piece left on the tarmac was a case with a bomb in it. Carefully, explosives experts took it away for examination.

The Senior Scientific Officer at the Home Office Branch of the Royal Armament Research and Development Establishment, Royal Arsenal East, Woolwich, is Mr Donald Lidstone, a man with over thirty years' experience of explosives. It was his task to take the Heathrow bomb apart and to note its make-up and any exceptional characteristics.

The "infernal machine" itself, in the jargon of the trade, was contained in an empty packet of Surf detergent. The explosive was a mixture of sugar and sodium chlorate, the ignition system was made up of two batteries wired to a North Sea gas lighter element. The timing mechanism was devised by the use of a cheap wrist watch. Simple ingredients, but when Mr Lidstone built a replica of the bomb it went off with dramatic effect. In the right ratio, mixtures of sugar and sodium chlorate can form sensitive and powerful explosives. From two pounds of it an intensely hot flame about 10 feet across roared up for a second and a half, giving off a large amount of black smoke, enough in an aircraft, Mr Lidstone observed, to impair a pilot's vision.

The Heathrow bomb had failed to go off because of a fault in the electro-mechanical works. But there was no doubt that it was the work of the First of May Group, part of a co-ordinated attack throughout Europe, and at Scotland Yard the Special Branch concentrated their inquiries in that direction. Not that at that stage they had a great deal to do. It was Mr Lidstone who was getting all the work. Just ten days after the Heathrow bomb, another unexploded device was brought down to his laboratory at Woolwich. This one had been found on the site of the new Paddington police station being built in Harrow Road.

At first there was nothing to connect the two. If anything, the Paddington bomb was the somewhat more sophisticated of the two. It had a continental detonator and two cartridges of French made explosives, Nitramite No. 19c, an extremely powerful blasting explosive consisting of TNT and ammonium nitrate.

But as Mr Lidstone went on with his analysis it became plain that there were strange similarities between the two bombs. The most obvious was the use in both of a gas lighter head of the type provided for professional use in installing North Sea gas appliances. It was something Lidstone had never come across before. Each device had two Ever Ready HP2 "high power" batteries, electrically connected in series. Again, these batteries were used to power North Sea gas igniters. Both bombs had pocket watches similarly modified to act as timing devices. Both bombs had a mixture of sugar and sodium chlorate. The same kind of Sellotape had been used to strap the various components together. All in all there was enough to suggest to Lidstone at any rate that the two bombs were likely to be related in some way. Maybe even made up by the same people or person.

At Scotland Yard, the Special Branch might have conceded the physical link between the bombs, but there was still no obvious ideological link between targets like Iberia Airlines and the site of Paddington police station. They did not know of any kind of coalition, alliance or merger between the First of May Group and the new libertarians. In fact, most of the details of bomb attacks were confined to the particular Metropolitan Police Division in which they occurred. Only the scientists at Woolwich would have had a chance to see any overall picture at that time, and they were not looking for one.

As for the bombers, for what was supposed to be a new departure in the politics of violence in Britain, the start had been singularly undramatic. Their first two bombs had failed to go off. The one at Heathrow was put down to some extremist group from abroad, the Paddington bomb got no publicity at all. Three months later, the next target—the office of Iberia Airlines in Regent Street—*was* slightly damaged by about half a pound of gelignite. There was scarcely any structural damage, but it was enough to get coverage on television and reports in the press. Then, just a few days later, at the end of August, came an attack that did seriously worry the authorities.

A bomb was left on the doorstep of the house in Roehampton of the Commissioner of the Metropolitan Police, Sir John Waldron. He was away at the time, but his daughter was in, and described the bang, the timing, and her reaction, though she saw nothing of the bombers themselves. Sir John was sent a letter saying he had been sentenced to death by the "revolutionary tribunal for crimes of oppression against many who are opposed to the capitalist regeime [sic] which you keep in power. Our executioner has been reprimanded for failing. We will make no further mistakes."

The letter was signed, "Butch Cassidy and the Sundance Kid".

It sounded like the work of cranks, some lunatic fringe, someone perhaps with a personal grudge against the police.

Meanwhile, the Commissioner himself was as curious as everyone else as to why anyone should want to blow him up. He asked for a briefing from the Special Branch, but there was little they could tell him. They certainly had no idea who might have been personally responsible, and the only plausible political motivation seemed to be resentment over the sentences handed out in the Garden House affair.

Earlier in the year there had been an incident at Cambridge University that had caused considerable controversy among students and the public at large. The details were fairly straightforward.

A dinner had been arranged at the Garden House Hotel in Cambridge to celebrate the end of a "Greek Week" in the city. It was promoted by the Greek national tourist board, an official agent of the Greek government. Tickets were £3 each: it was a formal occasion. Many of the guests—they had invited several Dons—were in evening dress. At around seven o'clock in the evening a crowd began to gather outside the hotel to protest about the dinner. As the guests arrived they had to run a gauntlet of abuse and anti-fascist slogans.

Suddenly a small group of students ran round to the back of the hotel, broke a plate-glass window and burst into the dining room, brandishing chairs in front of the startled guests. The local police were totally inadequate to deal with the situation, in numbers and in experience. They simply were not prepared for the strength of the demonstration, though they did have plenty of warning from the Special Branch in London about the possibilities of violence.

From the dozens of students arrested that night, sixteen were eventually sent for trial. Six of them were sentenced to between six and eighteen months in prison. The severity shocked the university authorities as much as it shocked the student body. Even moderate opinion was outraged. The proctors whose evidence had helped to convict the students were stunned by the length of the gaol terms. It was left to Lord Justice Sachs, in the Appeal Court, to put the Establishment view:

> When there is wanton and vicious violence of gross degree the court is not concerned whether it originates from gang rivalry or from political motives. It is the degree of the mob violence and the extent to which the public peace has been broken. It makes no difference whether the mob had attacked a first class hotel in Cambridge, or some dance hall frequented by the less well circumstanced.

In the press, leading articles discussed the judgement, the sentences, and the whole issue of political violence. Was the violence of the sentences greater than the violence of the affair itself? Was it over-reaction on the part of the Establishment? Could the severity of the sentences have been a motive for the bomb at Sir John Waldron's home? It was a possibility. And the theory gained more credibility from the bomb put down a week later at the London home of the Attorney General, Sir Peter Rawlinson.

The communiqué that went with it was not much help although it obviously came from the same source as the one sent out after the Commissioner's bomb. In shaky, childish printing it read: "You can dream up all the law and order you like. But remember—you are subject to our justice. He who liveth off the people by the people shall he die." It was signed with another film title—"The Wild Bunch".

At the time, neither attack received any publicity in the press or on television. The Press Association had issued a confidential memorandum to news editors asking them not to publish anything at the request of Scotland Yard until police inquiries were complete.

The people involved in the bombing were puzzled by this lack of publicity. After all, the bombs were supposed to be an "announcement" of a situation, and up to now there had been total silence. They were convinced that there was a conspiracy on the part of the authorities to keep the public in ignorance of all this urban guerrilla activity in case the idea should catch on.

But despite the press blackout on the Waldron and Rawlinson bombs, the campaign went on. At Heathrow on 26 September

it was impossible to conceal the details of the bomb in a
passenger lounge used by Iberia Airlines. No one was hurt in the
explosion but the bomb, hidden by a loaf of bread and a packet
of Weetabix in a green airline bag, caused immense confusion
at the airport. Again it was obviously First of May inspired,
and again it was timed to coincide with similar bombs on the
continent.

Concerted attacks were a First of May speciality. They had
been done successfully between Britain and the continent, now
it was the turn of three cities in Britain itself. Almost exactly at
the same time on the evening of 9 October, bombs went off at
the Italian Trade Centre in Cork Street, Mayfair, and two were
found unexploded at the Italian Consulates in Birmingham
and Manchester. Clearly, the team involved was substantial in
number and well co-ordinated. The targets they chose were also
intriguing.

The communiqués that went with the bombs made it plain
that the object had been to draw attention to the fate of
Giuseppe Pinelli, the Italian anarchist, who was the subject of
so much concern at the Grosvenor Avenue commune in North
London. Pinelli had been taken to Milan police station for
questioning a few days after the death of sixteen people in a
bomb attack on a city bank. During his interrogation, according
to the police, he threw himself out of a fourth floor window and
died instantly. Few people on the left in Italian politics believed
this explanation. They claimed that Pinelli had died under
interrogation and that his body had been thrown out of the
window. "The manner of my death cannot be concealed," went
the communiqué, and then the words "*Lotta Continua*"—the
name of an Italian revolutionary group well known to the
Special Branch in Britain.

As well as being closely involved with Italian anarchism
ever since fighting with anarchist partisans against Mussolini
during the war, Pinelli was the Black Cross representative and
organiser in Italy. He had obviously been in contact with
Stuart Christie, if not personally at least through corres-
pondence and an exchange of literature.

The Special Branch had been taking a passing interest in
Christie ever since his arrival back in Britain from prison in
Spain in 1967. Through Interpol they had learnt something of
his contacts in France and Spain, and though they had no

evidence, those contacts, they felt, came pretty close to the First of May Group. Christie was unquestionably suspect number one for the First of May attacks in England. After the Italian bombs, he was given the full surveillance treatment. His flat was raided, his friends were questioned, he was followed at work (converting appliances for North Sea gas). The Special Branch asked Albert Meltzer, a longstanding British anarchist, to use his influence to calm things down. But to calm *who* down—that was the real question, for Meltzer as much as for the "experts" in the Special Branch. And to make matters more complicated, the next set of events, the sequence of bomb and demonstration at the Miss World Contest, seemed to fit into no category at all.

On 19 November the BBC outside broadcast vans were parked round the side of the Royal Albert Hall ready to transmit the contest to the waiting millions all over Europe. At about two o'clock in the morning a group of youths, four or five of them, gathered quickly round one of the vans and slid their home-made bomb underneath it. The four ounces of TNT wrapped in a copy of *The Times* exploded a few minutes later, waking people in the large blocks of flats nearby. One of them got to her window in time to see the youths running down Kensington Gore towards Notting Hill.

The damage was not enough to delay the broadcast itself, but there was a slight interruption the following evening through an intervention from the balcony by a group of women's liberation supporters. They stood up and started to throw bags of flour towards the contestants on the stage. They were soon ejected from the Hall and, to a couple of jokes from Bob Hope, the show went on.

Among the demonstrators arrested at the Albert Hall were several who gave their address as 29 Grosvenor Avenue, the commune in North London. The Special Branch felt there must be a connection between the demonstration and the bomb, but how, why and what was still a mystery.

As a propaganda exercise, an expression of solidarity with the women's liberation movement, the Miss World bomb had been a success largely because of the nature of the target. There had been plenty of publicity on television and in the newspapers. Not so for the next attack though.

On 4 December a car sped past the Spanish Embassy in

Belgrave Square, and in an almost exact repeat of the attack on the American Embassy in Grosvenor Square three years earlier, a machine gun opened up. But whoever fired it was a poor shot. Only one bullet hit the Embassy itself. It made a hole in one of the front windows and, spent, dropped down behind some curtains. No one around, and there were very few people about at that time of night, heard a thing. Next day, therefore, there was no mention of the attack in the papers. The public at large was completely unaware of the incident. It took two full days for a cleaning lady to notice the bullet hole in the window, and for the police subsequently to find the remains of the bullet fired at the building.

In the meantime, the people behind the attack decided to deal with the uneven publicity they had been getting, in their own way. They were still convinced that the national press was deliberately suppressing news of their activities, and when they could not, they were distorting it. No doubt through the influence of the new libertarians in the group, who seemed to be gaining ground over the original First of May people despite their dependence on them for supplies, they settled on sending their communiqués to the "underground" press—to the *International Times* in particular (the First of May had always used the international news agencies or *The Times*).

To make sure everyone knew the communiqués were authentic, that they came from the right group, they devised a stamp made up by letters from a child's John Bull printing set. The name on it, thought up at a raucous, drunken Christmas party, would be "The Angry Brigade". The words were a rough translation of *Les Enragés*. The "Brigade" bit smacked slightly of the Spanish Civil War. It seemed an admirable composite.

The first time it was ever used was on a communiqué devised the day after the machine gunning of the Spanish Embassy— 5 December. It was too late to catch that week's edition of the *International Times*, so the world had to wait until 9 December to learn what was happening. It appeared in the paper as follows:

Brothers and sisters we expect the news of the machine gunning of the Spanish Embassy to be supressed by the bourgeois press. It's the third time over the last month that the systems dropped the mask of the so-called freedom of information and tried to hide the fact of its vulnerability. . . . They know the truth behind the BBC van the day before the Miss World farce: they know the truth behind the destruction of property of High Court Judges, they know the truth behind the four Barclays Banks which were either burned or badly destroyed, they also know that active opposition to their system is spreading.

The Angry Brigade doesn't claim responsibility for everything. We can make ourselves heard in one way or another. We machine gunned the Spanish Embassy last night in solidarity with our Basque brothers and sisters. We were careful not to hit the pigs guarding the building as representatives of British capital in fascist Spain. If Britain co-operates with France over this legal lynching by shutting the truth away we will take more careful aim next time.

SOLIDARITY AND REVOLUTION LOVE.

Communiqué the Angry Brigade.

In the same week, another communiqué arrived at the *International Times* with the same stamp.

Fascism and oppression will be smashed. (Spanish Embassy machine gunned Thursday.) High pigs, Judges, Embassies, Spectacles, Property.

That was communiqué two from the Angry Brigade, and as well as pulling together bomb attacks stretching back almost three years, it offered the first real clue to the political amalgam that had taken place.

"Fascism and oppression will be smashed. (Spanish Embassy machine gunned Thursday)"—the First of May Group, and the influence of the Spanish movement.

"High Pigs"—an obvious reference to the Waldron bomb. The phraseology reflected the American hippie scene.

"Judges"—presumably a reference to the Rawlinson bomb, though of course he was Attorney General, not the same thing, though he was regarded as part and parcel of the whole "repression industry".

"Embassies"—two were bombed, the Spanish and the American, not including the attempt on the Italian Consulates in Birmingham and Manchester. These were obviously to underline the group's international solidarity.

"Spectacles"—no doubt a reference to the Miss World contest, and the word that had sent the Special Branch sergeant scurrying to the few libertarian bookshops in London for the latest works of Debord and the Situationists. Once he had learned the vocabulary, the whole business of identifying the politics behind the communiqués became a lot easier. It also helped to narrow the field of suspects. There were not that many people around who had ever heard of the Situationist International, never mind who had ever read any of their works.

But although the kind of political sandwich offered by the communiqués helped to isolate the area of investigation (it is a proud boast of the Special Branch that throughout their inquiries they never raided "orthodox" extreme leftists) they were nevertheless worried by the apparent lack of political cohesion among the people doing the bombing. The Special Branch are naturally much happier dealing with organisations, with parties, with people who form themselves into units that can be penetrated, or at least from which individuals can be suborned. But the new revolutionary libertarians had nothing in the way of structures, no committees, branches, subscription lists. They moved about from commune to commune, joining one group, leaving and joining another. But by now events were moving so quickly that within a month of the first Angry Brigade communiqué, Britain was on the road to a permanent anti-urban guerrilla force.

In December, 1970, John Barker, who had begun to live permanently now with Hilary Creek, decided to move out of Notting Hill. He felt the district had become saturated with social workers and community activists, all busy "recuperating" the place. With £400 of Hilary Creek's money they bought a dilapidated house in Cannock Street in the slums of Moss Side, Manchester. They settled in about a week before Christmas.

Life at Cannock Street may not have been particularly comfortable but it was never dull. Barker described it as "a good scene. The joy of being in growing strength of us the people. It was real good there. Very relaxed." Seven people lived in the house, more or less permanently. They had meals together, spent a lot of time talking, arguing.

Barker and Creek took a lot of interest in the future of Moss Side itself. The area was due to be pulled down in the next few months as part of a council slum-clearance programme. But a group of architects at Manchester University had an alternative plan which showed that demolition was not really necessary. Barker arranged a protest meeting, and harassed the local councillors.

Cannock Street was also used by other people from London. They usually stayed a night or two, sometimes longer. Among the visitors just after New Year were Ian Purdie and Jake Prescott. The two men had got to know each other in Albany Prison on the Isle of Wight. Prescott was the classic "institutionalised" man. He was born in Dunfermline and after the death of his mother when he was six, he and his two sisters were brought up in an orphanage in Renfrewshire.

"My father never kept in touch with us. I ran away from the orphanage seven times because I was unhappy there. I was eleven when I committed my first offence, stealing a packet of dates from a shop."

At fourteen he stole a bicycle. At fifteen he appeared in court for receiving a stolen cigarette lighter and was sent to an approved school. At sixteen he absconded and after committing two housebreakings he was sent to Borstal.

Eventually he came to London and received more gaol sentences—four months, nine months, and twelve months, for various offences.

By 1966 Prescott was "hooked" on heroin and registered as an addict, but a year later his doctor disappeared.

"I was taking eight grains of heroin and other drugs every day, and I sold all my personal possessions to buy them.

"I picked up a rich-looking character and stole a whole lot of stuff from him, including a gun. The same night I went to Piccadilly and tried to contact a pedlar, but got arrested. Drugs were costing me £10 a day. At the police station I was told to turn out my pockets and I pulled out the gun. A policeman shouted, 'Watch out, he's got a gun.'

"One dived under a table, the others stood up against the wall. I ran out of the room. The gun was loaded."

Prescott was soon recaptured and sentenced to five and a half years for using a firearm to prevent his arrest and for drug offences. It was while he was serving this sentence that he met

Ian Purdie. For six weeks they shared the same cell, and eventually, according to Prescott, the same views.

"I had always accepted that I was a criminal, but that was a negative attitude and I began to realise that there were alternative ways of living."

Purdie talked about that alternative. He had quite a different background. He had been to a boarding school at Bembridge, not far from Albany, though he did say that on balance he preferred the prison. His family were comfortably off, middle-class radicals. Purdie had been active in the Vietnam Solidarity Campaign, but first came to the attention of the authorities during the 1969 Irish Civil Rights Campaign. He was arrested at one of their demonstrations and charged with throwing a petrol bomb at the Ulster Office in Savile Row. His sentence—nine months—landed him in Albany in the same cell as Jake Prescott.

To Purdie, Prescott seemed to represent everything that was wrong with society in general, and the penal system in particular. His single-handed struggle against authority since childhood, then his alienation as he sank deeper and deeper into difficulties without help, confirmed Purdie's revolutionary convictions.

Purdie had read and approved of the works of Vaneigem, and though never a member of the Kim Philby Dining Club, he shared the Situationists' admiration for him. He wrote from prison, "To me Philby is the real life Guy Fawkes—the guy who actually made it. It gives great satisfaction to me who's lived all his life in the UK to know that there was one guy who completely pissed on the upper echelons of the ruling class for years, devastating MI5 and MI6, and along with it the plans of imperial intrigue."

But the most important lesson Prescott learned from Purdie was that it was possible to change from struggling against society as an individual, which Prescott had done all his life, to struggling against society collectively.

"He realised," said Purdie, "that struggling collectively is more coherent, has more strength, has more power. And this leads further into struggling with his class . . . he came to realise there were different forms of struggle."

Before the two split up, Purdie told Prescott to get in touch with him when he was released, and this, almost immediately,

Prescott did. Soon the two men were joining in the general community activities in Notting Hill and North London, moving eventually to 29 Grosvenor Avenue.

Prescott slipped easily, and gratefully, into commune life. It was almost as if that was what he had been looking for all his life. Here was a group he could belong to, identify with, after a life of almost total institutionalised isolation. The people at Grosvenor Avenue were prepared to accept him for what he was, no questions asked, nothing much expected. Perhaps for the first time in his life Prescott felt safe.

Christmas and New Year 1970–71 was something of a high water mark for those hoping that the tide of libertarianism was about to wash over the whole country. The Government's "confrontation" with the unions was at its fiercest, with strikes, protests, and demonstrations almost every day. All over Britain libertarian activity was growing. The Squatting movement had spread dramatically, the Claimants Union now had a Federation of at least eighty branches, and for the tiny handful who had decided to complement all that with bombing, there had also been a measure of success. The authorities, the police, the Special Branch seemed a million miles away. Confidence was growing. There was even vague talk among some of going "underground" to escalate their activities, much as the Baader-Meinhoff Group had done in Germany. But in reality the options were narrowing, largely because of a substantial fraud conspiracy some of them began to engage in.

To people whose definitions of legality and illegality were their own, stealing cheque books and credit cards, mostly from students at the universities they visited, provided a lucrative and politically acceptable solution to the financial problems of full time revolutionary involvement. It was convenient, and safer, to take on the identity of those from whom they stole the documents. But it was also risky. Jim Greenfield was arrested at the begining of January, 1971, for dropping dud cheques. He was conditionally discharged. A few weeks later he was arrested again in possession of a car hired with a dud cheque. He was charged and went to court in the name of Caddick. He pleaded guilty and was fined. By some mischance, though his fingerprints were taken, his real identity was not discovered.

But just as the Baader-Meinhoff group in Germany had come unstuck when they started to involve themselves in "normal" criminality (in their case they paid money to underworld characters for advice on how to get guns, steal cars, forge documents. Some of these "advisers" were bought by the police, and turned into informers) so, in the end, Britain's new urban guerrillas were on a losing run when they started indulging in "straight" crime. The reason was pretty obvious. The police may not have known much about the politics of urban violence, but they knew only too well how to follow a trail of dud cheques. But tracking down fraud takes time, and the fact that nothing seemed to be happening to stop either the fraud activity or the bombing gave the people involved the confidence to organise an act of political violence on quite another scale.

CHAPTER FIVE

Habershon's inquiry gets under way . . . Suspects
. . . Christie and Purdie . . . The Prescott lead . . .
The Grosvenor Avenue commune

ONE THING DETECTIVE Chief Superintendent Habershon
had resolved from the start—the Carr bomb inquiry was to be
his inquiry. He let it be known, tactfully but firmly, that
whether it came from the CID, the Special Branch, the Fraud
Squad, the forensic people, or from members of the public, all
information had to be channelled through him. In effect,
Habershon became the focal point of the whole investigation.

At first, though, he did not have much to go on. There were
the bits and pieces collected from the debris at the Carrs' house
by the explosives expert, Major Henderson. They were sent
away to the Home Office forensic laboratory for analysis. The
house-to-house inquiries in the area did not reveal anything
substantial. The men from the fingerprint department could
not come up with anything either. The first positive clue came
into the Barnet Incident Room on the evening of 13 January.
Letters with a Barnet postmark had been received by *The Times*,
the *Guardian*, and the *Daily Mirror* that evening. Each one
contained a piece of paper with the words "Robert Carr got it
tonight. We're getting closer. The Angry Brigade. Communiqué 4."

No attempt, apparently, had been made to disguise the
handwriting on the envelopes, though the letters of the words
in the message inside were crudely constructed by lines drawn
with a ruler.

The first question Habershon had to answer for himself was
whether the communiqué was genuine or not. It could have
been a hoax, some kind of sick joke. Always after an incident of
this importance, with all the attendant publicity, the police
have this kind of problem. So, to help him make up his mind,
Habershon set his aides at Barnet to find out everything that
was already known about the Angry Brigade. Almost at once
they came up with the contents of communiqués one, two,

and three, each of which had been stamped with the printing set used on the Barnet communiqué. So the communiqués at least obviously came from the same people, people calling themselves the Angry Brigade, who were claiming responsibility for several bomb attacks and knowledge, at any rate, of others.

But it did not necessarily follow that the Angry Brigade stamp and the communiqués themselves came from the people involved in the incidents. It could still have been someone claiming credit for the attacks, say, after reading about them in the papers. What finally convinced Habershon that the people using the Angry Brigade stamp were the same as those involved in the attacks was the claim that they had machine gunned the Spanish Embassy in Belgrave Square. He reasoned it out like this: The communiqué containing the details of the attack arrived at the *International Times* on Monday, 7 December. It was dated 4 December. But when Habershon checked he found that the first the staff at the Embassy had known about the incident was on 6 December, two days later, when the cleaning woman had noticed a bullet hole in a window behind the curtains. So, as no one had even discovered the attack until well after the communiqué was written, the authorship had to be genuine, and it followed that all the other claims with the same stamp were likely to be authentic, too.

But there was another significant feature of the Spanish Embassy attack that Habershon began to ponder—the nature of the target itself. By now at his Barnet headquarters he had three Special Branch officers to help him, one of them an expert on anti-Franco activities in Britain. Habershon asked him to look into other recent anti-Franco attacks in Britain. The most recent had been at the offices of Iberia Airlines in Regent Street on 18 August, 1970. There were others that year, he discovered, some timed to coincide with explosions on the continent. But of course the Angry Brigade were not just claiming attacks on Spanish property. They made no secret of their protests against the Industrial Relations Bill and the Miss World contest, and when Habershon looked at some of the other bombs in 1970, it became plain from the forensic and explosives reports that a good few of them fitted the Angry Brigade pattern, including the incidents at the homes of Sir John Waldron and Sir Peter Rawlinson. Habershon also noted and sorted away for future reference that in several First of May bombs where explosive had been recovered intact, it was French, either Nitramite or Nitratex, both of which were unobtainable in Britain.

And that was not all. He had a laboratory report which showed that the same kind of French explosive had been used in a bomb placed outside the Department of Employment the previous December. So here was forensic link at least between the First of May Group and people who were interested in targets which had not the remotest Spanish connection. From these preliminary facts, within two or three days of the Carr bombs, Habershon had reached some tentative conclusions:

> I formed the view at that early stage that there existed in Britain a group of people of anti-Franco persuasion prepared to do bombing who had close contact with persons of similar mind on the continent, who themselves had access to French explosives. Secondly that this group had either extended its aims to include demonstrations against such things as police and government and authority in this country, or had joined forces with a second group who had those aims, and thirdly that the series of bombings with these new aims were being carried out under the label of the Angry Brigade.

Habershon was now convinced that there was a large-scale criminal conspiracy to cause explosions and that the only way to prosecute successfully those engaged in it was to "review the whole of the matters involved and extract every available piece of evidence and assistance from them".

The first and most obvious area of investigation was the life and times of Stuart Christie. By now the Special Branch dossier on him was pretty substantial. Partly because he lived in the same house as the two men arrested after the First of May bomb at the Bank of Bilbao, Christie was suspected of extensive contacts with the group. He had also been sent by the Anarchist Federation of Britain to the International Anarchist Congress at Carrara in Italy in August, 1968. He shared rooms with Daniel Cohn-Bendit, who was there to represent the 22 March movement.

Christie himself, of course, has never disguised his anarchist views. With Albert Meltzer he had published an exposition of anarchist theory in a book: *The Floodgates of Anarchy*. Through pamphlets, articles, and personal demonstration he had achieved a certain notoriety. But more important, to Habershon's thinking, was Christie's "previous" involvement with bombs.

Through Interpol, Habershon got hold of details of the bomb-making kit which had been supplied to Christie to take to Madrid as part of a plan to blow up Franco. The contents of his rucksack when he was arrested consisted of MacCartney serum bottles with pierced and unpierced caps, paper discs for use inside the caps, and instructions about fuse delay lengths. There was a bag of potassium chlorate, five packets of gelatine high explosive, and eight detonators. Working from that and other information supplied by Interpol, Habershon began to build up a comprehensive picture of the First of May Group and its activities. The Special Branch provided him with Alberola's name as the Group's public relations man, and, they suspected, much more. One person in Britain they believed was in regular contact with Alberola was Stuart Christie.

Habershon had already come to the conclusion that Christie was a possible member of a bombing conspiracy. But he needed evidence. These vague Special Branch hypotheses would never stand up in a court of law. But one piece of information came Habershon's way that might prove useful. Stories about the police looking for "a young Scottish anarchist" had begun to appear in the newspapers, with Christie the obvious inference. The *Daily Mirror* had even gone so far as to offer £10,000 reward for information leading to the arrest of anyone connected with the Carr bomb attack.

On 16 January, a Mrs Lisa Byer was brought to Barnet police station for questioning, and eventually she made a statement. She said she worked as a barmaid at a pub in Ruislip, and among her "regulars" were Stuart Christie and several of the men who worked with him on a local gas conversion contract. According to Mrs Byer, Christie asked her to go out with him. She said they went for meals in Camden Town, Queensway, and Notting Hill. Often he made calls at houses in the area, but she herself never went in. She was left sitting in the car outside. Most of the time, she said, Christie was delivering pamphlets, but on two occasions, she told Habershon, he delivered some ammunition.

On the first occasion he'd called for me at my house at about six o'clock and had driven me in his van to Camden Town. As I got into the van I noticed a small parcel wrapped in newspaper lying on the passenger seat. Christie moved it to the parcel shelf. I got in and being nosey, opened the parcel. I saw that it was a clip of bullets and asked Christie what it was. He said it was a magazine. I asked him what it was for and what he was going to do with it, and he told me not to be so nosey.

Mrs Byer mentioned another occasion when Christie had delivered some bullets, but when Habershon asked her whether he had ever mentioned explosives, she said the only time was when he had wanted to know if any explosives were kept in the armoury at her husband's base at Ruislip. That was all.

Mrs Byer's statement obviously increased Habershon's suspicions about Christie, but he decided against interviewing him at this stage. Instead, he ordered further surveillance of Christie and of some of his friends. Two squad cars were permanently parked outside Christie's house. Everywhere he went he was followed. Christie himself was convinced that his phone calls were monitored, that his mail was opened. He took what evasive action he could. He knew very well that he was under suspicion, and he was anxious that his friends should escape a similar fate. He decided to lodge some of his papers and his address book with a friend. But the police found it, or stole it, as Christie later claimed, and Habershon studied the names in it closely. He ordered inquiries to be made about everyone mentioned, including John Barker. As Habershon later put it, the diary amounted to a "glossary of revolutionaries", both in Britain and abroad. The Paris telephone number of Alberola's girl friend Ariane Gransac was there, and so too was that of Giuseppe Pinelli, the Italian Black Cross organiser whose death had occasioned the three bombs in London, Birmingham and Manchester on 9 October, 1970.

So Stuart Christie was suspect number one, and just a few days after the Carr bombs the papers were carrying stories about the police looking for a young Scots anarchist. It was a leak that pleased neither Habershon nor Christie. The inference was obvious. Still, using much the same technique of looking for a similar *modus operandi*, for "evidence of similar facts", Habershon arrived at suspect number two.

Ian Purdie's record was soon dug out of the files, and although his offence had been throwing a petrol bomb, the motivation, Habershon considered, was the same as that behind the Carr bombs. He felt it would be worth talking to Purdie at least. So on 15 January, three days after the Barnet bombs, the flat Purdie was thought to be living in was raided. He was not there, but five days later, he came forward voluntarily and gave Habershon a statement to the effect that he had travelled to Edinburgh on the 12th to stay with friends in South Queensferry. They supported Purdie's alibi, although they "revealed", as Habershon put it, that he had left them to go to Manchester on the 14th, returning to Edinburgh on the 17th and going on to London the following day.

All these movements and dates were duly noted down by Habershon, who was also beginning to build some kind of picture of the kind of people he was dealing with. Purdie's friends in particular were "difficult", largely unco-operative. Purdie himself was tough minded, aggressive, conscious of his rights, not likely to give much away even if there was anything to give. But the break Habershon was looking for was on the way.

On 20 January, eight days after the Carr bomb attack, one Jake Prescott was walking down Talbot Road in Notting Hill a little unsteadily. Drunk or drugged, it didn't matter, it was enough to draw the attention of two policemen in uniform who were on a routine patrol. They took him along to the police station where a search revealed some cannabis resin and three cheque books. From the start, it was obvious that the cheque books did not belong to Prescott. In fact, two of them turned out to have been stolen the day before from a student's room at Oxford University. The other had been stolen from the address at Roehampton, where he was supposed to have been paroled.

To the police at Notting Hill this was all pretty routine stuff. People were being pulled in for drugs every day. There was nothing exceptional about the cheques either, but because of his record, Prescott was sent to Brixton prison on remand to wait for the magistrates' hearing. He was put into a cell along with two other prisoners, back in the environment in which he had spent most of his adult life. But the last three months of liberty had had a profound effect on Prescott. He could not resist talking about it, encouraged by one of his cell mates in particular who was an informant of the local CID Inspector.

Prisoner "A", as he was described later at the trial, was inside for dishonest handling and other offences. No doubt hoping for some kind of remission, he contacted Inspector Peck and told him that he had some information about the Carr bomb attack and that he wanted to see Mr Habershon. Mr A was due to appear on remand at Camberwell magistrates' court on the morning of 3 February. Habershon went there to interview him. In all, the two met three times, and on each occasion Mr A provided Habershon with more information.

In effect, Mr A was saying that Prescott, at that time totally unknown to Habershon or anyone else dealing with the case, had admitted to being concerned in the Carr bombing, and also with the bomb at the Department of Employment and at the BBC van at the Miss World contest. Prescott had described in some detail the two Carr bombs, how they had been placed, and how they were made up. As none of this had been publicised, only someone with first-hand knowledge could have known about it. Habershon realised that Prescott could not have been making the whole thing up as a kind of boast to impress his cellmates. But to check out Prescott and all the bits and pieces of information Prisoner A had reported would take time and resources. If it turned out to be wrong, if Prisoner A was making any of it up for his own benefit, it could prejudice the rest of the inquiries and waste valuable time and money. On the other hand, Habershon did not have much else to go on, so he made up his mind to follow the Prescott lead through.

As a first step, Habershon asked for all Prescott's personal effects to be sent from Brixton to Barnet for examination. As well as the three cheque books found on him by the Notting Hill police, there was a forged student union membership card and, most important of all, his address book. Habershon had a feeling he had seen the writing in it somewhere else—on the envelopes, he suspected, sent to the newspapers with the Carr bomb communiqués. He got a handwriting expert up to Barnet to look at the address book. Straight away, he gave a verbal opinion that the envelope and the address book were written by the same hand. If this could be proved forensically, it would be the first piece of concrete evidence in the case so far.

The news gave a much needed boost to the morale of the team at Barnet investigating the bombings. It gave them heart for their next daunting task—to check out all the names and addresses in Prescott's book. From that list, and from what Prisoner A had told him, Habershon was beginning to construct a comprehensive pattern of acquaintanceship. But he needed stronger evidence than names in a book. He had to prove association as well.

On 3 February, a fortnight after he had been picked up in Notting Hill, Prescott was let out on bail. Habershon had his every move watched. The flats, bedsitters, houses he went to, the people he met, were all noted down and checked against the names in Christie's address book, as well as his own. The address that appeared to be emerging as the most significant in the inquiries (it was certainly the most frequent) was 29 Grosvenor Avenue. It was Prescott's first call after his release on bail. Habershon staked the place out, or in more formal police parlance "caused surveillance to be kept on the occupants, and for inquiries to be made concerning them".

"I learned," he said, "that this four-storeyed address housed persons who were extremely active full time in revolutionary politics, and that a large amount of printing in support of various causes in this field was being carried on there, prominent amongst which was opposition to the Industrial Relations Bill, and promulgating the more extreme Women's Liberation views."

Habershon also discovered that on 11 February three of the women living at Grosvenor Avenue were to appear at a resumed hearing at Bow Street Magistrates' court on charges against them arising out of the demonstration against the Miss World contest in November.

Habershon guessed that a large number of the girls' supporters and friends would be at the court, so he arranged for members of the Barnet team to attend the hearing and at the same time posted more men to watch 29 Grosvenor Avenue. Habershon himself left Barnet for Bow Street court in good time for the hearing. At about one o'clock one of the detectives keeping observation on Grosvenor Avenue saw a group of women leave, presumably to attend the Bow Street hearing. Then, an hour later, out came Prescott and a Dutchman, Jan Oudenaarden, who was also living there. The two men went along to the Weavers Arms public house in Newington Green Road, followed by two detectives.

The news that Prescott had been seen leaving Grosvenor Avenue was phoned to Habershon at Bow Street where the hearing was just about to begin. He told the detectives waiting outside the Weavers Arms to arrest the two men and take them to Barnet police station to wait for his return. He himself went inside the court room to see what was happening.

As he had expected, the public seats were filled with Grosvenor Avenue supporters. In fact there were so many that they overflowed on to the landing and stairs outside the court. As people milled about all over the building the four defendants surrendered their bail and took their places in the dock. Of the four, only one was represented by counsel; the others were defending themselves, which tended to add to the confusion. Soon the proceedings degenerated into a total shambles, and the Magistrate, Mr Rees, decided to cut the whole thing short, remanding all four in custody until the following day.

While the Magistrate was trying to sort out the confusion in the court, outside Habershon got together with the other officers in his team to try to decide which of the large number of people at the court might be of help to his inquiries. He decided eventually to arrest four women he knew had connections with Grosvenor Avenue—Jane Grant, Sarah Wilson, Sarah Martin, and Sue Bruley. They were put into a police van in the street outside the court, and driven straight to Barnet for "questioning as to their complicity in the Carr bombing". Habershon did not go with them. He had other work to do at Grosvenor Avenue itself.

When he got there, a search was already under way with a warrant under the Explosive Substances Act. Habershon took over.

The raid on Grosvenor Avenue on the afternoon of 11 February was really the beginning of the bitter battle between the police and the people who comprised the political and social context Habershon was now convinced the Angry Brigade sprang from. In a sense it was easy for him. He could get an overall picture of the kind of society he was dealing with; but to the dozens of young policemen and women in his team it was all a total mystery. Most of them, even those who had been on the drug squad, were dealing with a life-style they had never come across before. They were shocked by the conditions they saw in the communes they raided. They could not begin to understand how people could live that way by choice.

In one place they raided, there was no wall round the lavatory. As the detectives were sifting through books and papers in the flat, one of the girls living there sat on the lavatory pan and began to "crap". If it was meant as a symbolic act it was lost on the police, who saw it simply for what it was. But as an illustration of what they were up against, it was perfect to tell in the Tank, the bar in the basement of Scotland Yard. As the incident took on more embellishments, it added to and confirmed the prejudices that already existed among the police against the so-called alternative society.

As for the "communards" themselves, as the police began to call them, they looked on the police as pigs, the filth. To justify their vilification, they pointed to the way the police treated them. The violence, the damage, the way they left everything in chaos after a search. The dogs they brought along to sniff out explosives were an intrusion, the questioning, an insult.

The antagonism and mutual incomprehension was at its worst when the police, mostly working class or lower middle class in origin, who accepted the values that society expected them to uphold, personally confronted a group of people from the same social background, but who had rejected those values utterly. To Habershon, though, the answer was quite straightforward:

> I had to get amongst these people, because responsibility for the bombings clearly lay in that area. I had to get among them, and I had to put my men among them. If people go about preaching violence and revolution and a bombing of that sort occurs in that context then they must expect to be the object of police attention.

As well as the women he knew were living at Grosvenor Avenue, Habershon established that a number of men were permanent residents, and that most of them had been at Cambridge University and formed the nucleus of the Cambridge Situationist group. Some had been members of the Kim Philby Dining Club.

Habershon, of course, knew from the Special Branch that

all the people living at Grosvenor Avenue were engaged in
revolutionary politics. Now he saw it for himself.

> Large quantities of revolutionary leaflets and pamphlets
> were evidently issuing from the well-equipped printing press
> which occupied the front basement room. From my examina-
> tion of the premises it was obvious that they were the living
> and business quarters of some dozen or so persons who were
> wholly occupied in promulgating revolutionary ideas,
> including that of the Claimants Union.

Habershon also noted that one room upstairs was given over
wholly to matters concerned with Italian anarchist activities,
and in particular he saw "evidence of extreme interest in the
person Pinelli and the Italian slogan, *Lotta Continua*"; they'd
both figured of course in the communiqués sent out after the
Italian bombings on 9 October, 1970. There was also an
abundance of evidence of extreme interest in opposition to the
Industrial Relations Bill and in militancy in Women's Liberation matters. After he had looked through all the paperwork at
the house, Habershon tried to question the people there. "It
proved fruitless," he said. The antagonism was complete.

When his search of Grosvenor Avenue was finished
Habershon went back to Barnet police station to interrogate
the four girls who had been taken there earlier from Bow Street
court, and of course to interview Prescott and the Dutchman,
Oudenaarden. By now the girls had been in custody for about
nine hours and they were, to say the least, angry. To
Habershon's questions they were in the main evasive. But they
did confirm that Prescott and Purdie had been staying at
Grosvenor Avenue, and that arrangements for the Miss World
demonstration had indeed been made there. All four gave their
alibis for the time of the Carr bombing, wrote out the three
addresses which were on the Carr communiqué envelopes, and
around midnight were allowed to go home.

As for Prescott, he denied having anything to do with any
bombing. But he could give no clear indication of his movements on 12 January, except to say he was with a girl whose
name he gave to Habershon. In his interrogation, Prescott got
himself into all sorts of difficulties. At one stage, he almost
admitted being involved in the bombings, only refusing to name

his confederates. At first he denied addressing the three envelopes, but later conceded that he might have written them without knowing what they were to be used for. He admitted possession of the stolen cheque books. He said he had used one of them to get three return tickets to Manchester on 13 January, the day after the Carr bombs. This reference to Manchester opened up a new line of inquiry. Prescott said he had stayed there in a commune that was like the one at Grosvenor Avenue. He did not know what the address was except that it was somewhere in Moss Side. Again using a stolen cheque book, he had bought toys, food, clothes and drink for the people living there. Prescott also revealed that when he returned from Manchester to London, he had gone along to Liverpool Street Station to buy a ticket to Wivenhoe for Anna Mendelson, who, he said, was staying at Grosvenor Avenue.

Though the names Prescott was mentioning did not mean anything to Habershon at this stage, he encouraged him to give them. Sometimes, Prescott could only give Christian names. In Manchester, for example, were Kay, Hilary, Joe, Chris and John. All of them were noted down for reference and cross reference. Prescott talked about the Notting Hill People's Association, run by a Greek called, he thought, Mike Topolopolis. This interested Habershon especially because he had already heard about the People's Association and the Greek running it from Prisoner A. It served once more in Habershon's mind to corroborate Prisoner A's account as a true version of the prison cell conversations.

Next, after this general line of questioning, Habershon took Prescott through the names in his address book one by one. Who were they, what were they doing, where did they live? One address to emerge in this way was 14 Cannock Street. Habershon suggested to Prescott that this might be the address in Manchester of the commune he had talked about, but could not remember exactly where it was.

"Yes," said Prescott, "that's it. I didn't say so before because I didn't want to get anyone into trouble."

The Cannock Street address was immediately telexed to Manchester police. They arranged a raid for the following day. John Barker, who was there, has described the result.

In a way the atmosphere of the house changed after that

raid. We had the feeling that we could be raided at any time, taken in at any time, questioned at any time and in fact the feeling that we would get more and more aggravation from the Manchester police. In fact it did happen. We used to get these unofficial visits. It would be dramatic to say that we felt in a state of siege, but it was certainly a feeling that the house was hardly our own any more.

For Habershon, though, the most interesting section of his interrogation of Prescott was what he had to say about his relations with Ian Purdie. Prescott talked quite freely about it, about how Purdie had introduced him to the people at Grosvenor Avenue, about how they came to stay there, and about how they kicked Purdie out eventually because they thought he was a terrorist.

After many hours of questioning over three days, Habershon felt that he had got all he was going to get out of Prescott, so he decided to charge him with conspiracy to cause explosions under the 1883 Explosive Substances Act. Prescott faced a maximum sentence of twenty years.

CHAPTER SIX

*The first arrests . . . The protests grow . . . Angry
Brigade bombs and communiqués*

HABERSHON WAS NOW convinced that Prescott had been
involved in the Carr bomb attack and no doubt in some of the
others. As a result, he began to concentrate his inquiries on
everyone Prescott had met in the short period since he had left
Albany Prison in September, 1970.

> I also took the view that he was such a politically naïve and
> previously uninvolved person that any person who could be
> found to have influenced him in any way during his period at
> liberty up to and since the Carr bombing must be heavily
> suspect as being also involved.

That was how Ian Purdie "came into the frame". To
Habershon he was clearly Prescott's mentor and constant
companion since his release from Albany.

"I was quite satisfied from the other evidence I had about
Purdie that he was a co-conspirator not only in the bombings,
but in the fraud, too."

Habershon put in hand inquiries to trace and arrest Purdie,
and meantime went up to Scotland to follow up the names and
addresses Prescott had mentioned there.

While he was on his trip to the North, thanks largely to the
initiative of the Dunfermline police, Habershon had another
break. During a drug raid in their district, the local police had
found a handwritten letter from Prescott to a girl who was now
living in Edinburgh. When they heard about Prescott's arrest,
they sent Habershon a copy.

"I found it most interesting," he said.

The letter had been written from Grosvenor Avenue, and
described the life there. Purdie and Oudenaarden were
mentioned. There was some cryptic talk about drugs and the
theft of some turkeys which they had eaten at the commune.
But what interested Habershon particularly was a reference to
Prescott having come to Edinburgh for something specific and

having got it. That, Habershon felt, could well have been explosives.

Habershon's Scottish trip gave him another lead. During his rounds of Edinburgh's anarchist scene, surprisingly large for the size of the city, he discovered that Prescott had been engaged at one time to a girl called Irene Jamieson. She had been a regular visitor to Albany prison to see him, and he in turn had written her many letters from prison. When he got back to London Habershon interviewed Irene Jamieson at length. She told him that she had noted a change in Prescott's attitude to society in general during his time in Albany. She produced one particular letter from Prescott in which he expressed some especially violent political intentions. Jamieson said she had also passed messages to Ian Purdie in Albany from a man called Jerry Osner. Some of them dealt with arrangements for getting anarchist literature into the prison. Miss Jamieson also told Habershon that Purdie and Osner seemed to be playing an increasingly predominant role in Prescott's life. So much so that in the end she broke off their engagement and stopped seeing him altogether.

Slowly Habershon was amassing a great deal of background material about a circle of people, some of whom he was convinced were concerned in the bombings. He now had the results of the research and inquiry into the contents of Prescott's address book. There were fifty-five names in it, thirty-six of whom were associated together "in the pursuit of revolutionary politics". Seventeen of these had contacts with Grosvenor Avenue. Nine were friends of Prescott in Scotland. The remaining ten could not be put into any category. He also had seven addresses in London, one in Manchester, and one in Wivenhoe, all of which he defined as "communes", and with each was a list of people who visited them.

None of this material was of real evidential value. But on 4 March, Habershon received the tip-off he had been waiting for. Ian Purdie had been seen using an address in South London, in Tyneham Road, Battersea. He sent his officers to pick him up, with a warrant under the Explosives Act to search the place. But just as the police were reaching the front door, Purdie ran out of the back, over the garden fence and on to some waste ground. After a short chase, he was caught and taken to Barnet for questioning.

Prescott was the sort of man Habershon was used to dealing with, a petty criminal who had been fair game for the police all his life. Purdie was in an altogether different category. To start with, he was a much stronger character, more intelligent, certainly a match for Habershon in argument, and he knew precisely how to "stand on his rights". In two days of interrogation, Purdie made no admissions, nor did he offer any explanation about why he had run away from Tyneham Road, or about what he had been doing over the past few weeks since Prescott's arrest. In fact Purdie said virtually nothing at all. Nevertheless, on the afternoon of 7 March, he was charged with conspiring with Prescott and others unknown to cause explosions.

The arrest of Prescott and Purdie in no way inhibited the political activity of their friends. There was of course no reason why it should, even if some of the raids were intimidating. One day towards the end of February, a notice went up on the wall of the office of *Frendz*, the underground newspaper, asking anyone interested in putting out a new kind of libertarian newspaper to attend a meeting in Liverpool on 27 February. About one hundred and thirty people actually went. They represented a whole range of political groups—community action, Claimants unions, shop floor organisations, schools groups. Among those present were Jim Greenfield, Anna Mendelson, and up from Cannock Street, John Barker and Hilary Creek. Barker explained the purpose of the occasion:

As I understood it the first meeting was not specifically about a newspaper, but was more general than that. How to work out what all sorts of people who were doing the same kind of things as ourselves were moving towards. That was how to create some kind of network between all these different things in local areas of communities. And at Liverpool the discussion started off that way. In fact there was a kind of argument as to whether we should do a newspaper or whether it would be better to do duplicated sheets from different people in different areas which would be sent to one central point and then . . . sent out again. But in fact we decided on a newspaper because mainly a newspaper is more concrete. It is something which is easier to hand around.

The paper was to be called *Strike*. There was to be no editorial board. No one person was to define what was to go into it. The contents would be decided by the people who wrote for it. Anna Mendelson put it this way:

> I was sick of reading the alternative papers to the big national press that were available. I think that there were very real things that were happening which I wanted to write about. Not inside any organisation at all. Not put out a paper which had a party line, but a paper that would bring together a lot of things that people were doing.

When *Strike* did eventually get off the ground, Greenfield, Mendelson, Barker and Creek all contributed to it with various articles. Not without a touch of irony, Greenfield and Mendelson contributed a piece on Judges and the Law—the so-called Repression Industry. There was also a plea on behalf of Prescott and Purdie.

But all that was some way off. On the night in question, after the meeting in Liverpool, Greenfield and Mendelson with three friends drove to Widnes, Greenfield's home town, not far away. They stopped for a drink and parked the car, which had been hired by Greenfield with a stolen credit card, on a forecourt outside a pub. One of the customers thought they looked a bit suspicious and telephoned the police. The pub was almost closing by the time they got there. They asked Greenfield who he was, and he said his name was Kellaway, a failed student at Essex University now doing some journalistic work in Widnes. But he couldn't produce any documents to say how he had obtained the car outside, so all five were taken along to Widnes police station. They were searched, and in their possession was found a cheque book stolen from Essex University, a quantity of cannabis, and some amphetamines. All five were bailed to Colchester police station under false names and addresses.

Essex University was rapidly becoming one of the focal points of the inquiry. Habershon, who had asked for everything that was known in criminal records about everyone he suspected, found that Greenfield had stolen two turkeys from a small-holding at Wivenhoe the previous November. He had been dealt with at the local court, and fined. Again during a raid on Cannock Street, police found a typewriter stolen from Essex University, where of course Mendelson and Creek had been students. Habershon was now getting plenty of information about his suspects, but it was largely to do with fraud and other minor offences, nothing about the bombings, and they were continuing.

In the early hours of 19 March, there was an explosion at the Ford Motor Company's offices at Gants Hill in Essex. The only significant clue was a report by a resident in Grosvenor Avenue that there had been a lot of coming and going by people in cars outside number 29 during the night. Habershon accordingly arranged for yet another raid on the place, with a warrant once again under the Explosive Substances Act. His men went through the place meticulously. Not a trace of explosives, but while the search was going on a girl drove up in a blue Volkswagen, parked it outside, and came into number 29. After some debate among themselves about the proprieties of it, the police decided to include the Volkswagen in their search, and it was taken away to Holborn for forensic examination. Again, there was no trace of explosives, but someone noticed that one of the keys they had found in the car looked rather unusual. The Special Branch checked it out and found that it came from a left luggage locker at Euston Station.

On Habershon's instructions they went along to the station, opened the locker and found inside two holdalls of material that could only be described as a "fraud" kit. There were stolen cheque books, Barclaycard application forms, banking documents, and some private papers belonging to a German, Wolf Seeberg, who by now had rung the police, ostensibly from Germany, saying the car was his and could he have it back.

Habershon decided to set a trap. He told his men to put back the contents of the locker and to keep a twenty-four hour watch on it. Sure enough, the following day a girl walked up to the attendant and explained that she had lost her key and could he provide another one. He did, and just as she was in the process of opening the locker, two detectives stepped forward and arrested her. A few days later, she was charged with dishonest handling, and let out on bail.

As for Seeberg, the phone call he said was from Germany was traced to an address in the Provisional IRA stronghold in Andersonstown in Belfast. It was the home of the Provisional

leaders, Rita and Jerry O'Hare. One night, at some considerable risk to themselves, a squad of police raided the house to
pick up Seeberg. They found him in bed with the girl who had
been arrested at Euston a few days earlier.

Seeberg was brought back to London, and at Albany Street
police station, the nearest to Euston, he was charged in relation
to the material found in the locker. By the end of March, it
was plain that a large scale concerted fraud conspiracy was
taking place among a group of people Habershon suspected of
the bombing.

> It was evident [he said] that these persons and their
> associates whose identities I was learning were and had been
> for some time wholly engaged in revolutionary political
> activities of various sorts and that the majority had no
> visible means of income. It was a reasonable assumption to
> come to that they were subsidising and financing their various
> activities from the proceeds of fraud.

As neither he nor his officers at Barnet had the time to investigate
the frauds in any depth, he asked for, and got, his own Fraud
Squad, based at Scotland Yard under Detective Inspector
George Mould.

Meanwhile at Barnet the team continued to prepare their
case against Prescott and Purdie, who had been remanded in
custody until 22 April.

Predictably enough, the way Habershon was conducting his
inquiries began to draw increasing criticism. Hundreds of
people had experienced police raids. Some were well known in
the pop world, others were articulate, vocal and influential.
In the Commons on 18 March, Mr Clinton Davis put a question
down for the Home Secretary, Mr Maudling, asking why so
many people had been detained at Barnet police station and
then released. At that stage twenty-five had been taken in for
questioning and not charged. One man was held for forty-eight
hours, another for twenty-four hours. There were also
complaints about solicitors not being allowed to see their
clients.

One of the most deeply felt objections was to the way the
police were using warrants to search for explosives, when,

according to the complainants, they knew very well none were there. In other words, many people felt the police were using explosives warrants as an excuse for indiscriminate searching. The National Council for Civil Liberties complained to the Home Secretary that this, in effect, was against the Judges' Rules, the guide-lines laid down for police investigations. They cited as another example of the way the Judges' Rules had been flouted the case of the four women taken from Bow Street court to Barnet for questioning about the Carr bombing. They were taken there from the court precincts against their will. In no sense, said the NCCL, were they "voluntarily helping the police with their inquiries". The NCCL provided money from their Defence Fund to help the women take out an action against the police for false imprisonment and assault.

At the start of the Prescott/Purdie committal proceedings there was a row between Prescott's defence lawyer, Mr Arnold Rosen, and the police. He successfully applied to the magistrate to have detectives ordered out of court during the proceedings, contrary to normal custom which allows the officer in charge of the case to sit in to assist the prosecution. Mr Rosen also objected to an attempt by the police to search him as he entered the court.

> I do not like an attempt to have a search made on me for any recorders, cameras, or whatever else the police may think it would be wrong to have in court. I understand that the police are acting with the best will in the world to protect people attending the hearing, but I take it it won't be necessary for me to make mention of this fact at any time in the future.

The Magistrate agreed that it was beneath the dignity of a member of the Bar that he should be searched unless there was any good reason. But Habershon had other things to do at the hearing besides arguing with cantankerous defence lawyers. He was anxious to check the identity of everyone who came to attend the hearing and to find out who went to see the two prisoners in custody. People who sat in the public gallery were also noted and checked against names already known. Habershon was also as keen to find out who did not come as who did. He made a list of those who he felt were conspicuous by their absence. They included Greenfield, Mendelson, Creek, and Stuart Christie.

In his original report to the Director of Public Prosecutions on 19 March, Habershon had suggested that the prosecution for conspiracy to cause explosions should take in fourteen incidents beginning with the First of May attack on the Spanish Embassy in Belgrave Square in March, 1968, right up to the Carr bombing. One of the reasons he was able to include such a wide spread of explosions was some remarkable work done by Mr Howard Yallop, Mr Lidstone's boss at the Home Office Branch of the Royal Armament Research and Development Establishment at Woolwich.

Yallop had developed a technique of analysis so sensitive that he could tell what chemical substances had been used in a bomb, even after it had gone off. He was able to tell from the traces left behind on, say, a burnt piece of wood or tangled metal exactly what kind of explosive had been used and what its ingredients were. Through this method, and by weighing up other common factors, he and Habershon had put together a list of explosions, fourteen in all, which they believed were linked into a single "associated" set. This meant that explosions in the "set" could be attributed as a whole to a single person or group of persons.

In a sense Yallop's task of looking for scientific associations between explosions had complemented Habershon's task of looking for political associations between people. But in the event, when the scheme was referred to Treasury Counsel, Mr Matthew, he advised against it, suggesting in turn a conspiracy that took in only five explosions—at the Waldron and Rawlinson homes, at the Miss World contest, the DEP in St James's Square, and at the home of Mr Robert Carr. Habershon's original conspiracy charge was accordingly amended, and the committal proceedings went ahead on that basis.

But both Habershon and Yallop felt that the shortened version of the conspiracy would be injurious to the Crown's case, and in fact during the hearing, in the cross-examination of Yallop, the association of the fourteen incidents and the facts about each were put in evidence before the examining Magistrate. And so the opening round in the long, contentious legal battle began on 27 May, 1971, with the committal of Purdie and Prescott for trial at the Old Bailey.

But just because Purdie and Prescott were in custody, awaiting trial, Habershon had no illusions that he had smashed the Angry Brigade. Quite the contrary, with Prescott and Purdie now a cause in themselves, their activities seemed to be increasing. The communiqué following the bombing at the Ford offices at Gants Hill bore the authentic stamp, and claimed responsibility once more for the bombs at the homes of Carr, Rawlinson and Waldron. To Habershon, it was evident that there were "still persons attaching this label to themselves who were prepared to pursue the aims of conspiracy with which Prescott and Purdie were charged, and who still possessed the capability and determination to cause dangerous and lethal explosions for their political ends".

Those "political ends" were now becoming a lot clearer to Habershon. The Special Branch officers working on the case were collecting vast amounts of material, most of it printed on privately-owned duplicating machines. There were leaflets, pamphlets, crudely prepared booklets, posters, articles in the underground press, particularly in the *International Times*, *Frendz*, and *Time Out*. But above all, and most important evidentially, there were the communiqués stamped with the Angry Brigade's John Bull printing set. One that interested the Special Branch particularly was found during a raid on the "Agit Prop" commune in Muswell Hill. It was a photostat copy bearing the authentic Angry Brigade stamp, and it read:

FELLOW REVOLUTIONARIES . . .
We have sat quietly and suffered the violence of the system for too long. We are being attacked daily. Violence does not only exist in the army, the police, and the prisons. It exists in the shoddy alienating culture pushed out by T.V. films, and magazines, it exists in the ugly sterility of urban life. It exists in the daily exploitation of our Labour, which gives big bosses the power to control our lives and run the system for their own ends.

How many Rolls Royce . . . how many Northern Irelands . . . how many anti-Trade Union bills will it take to demonstrate that in a crisis of capitalism the ruling class can only react by *attacking* the people *politically*? But the system will never collapse or capitulate by itself. More and more workers now realise this and are transforming union consciousness into offensive political militancy. In one week, one million workers were on strike . . . Fords, Post Office, B.E.A., oil delivery workers . . .

Our role is to deepen the political contradictions at every level. We will not achieve this by concentrating on "issues" or by using watered down socialist platitudes. In Northern Ireland the British army and its minions has found a practising range: the C.S. gas and bullets in Belfast will be in Derby and Dagenham tomorrow.

Our attack is violent . . .

Our violence is organised.

The question is not whether the revolution will be violent. Organised militant struggle and organised terrorism go side by side. These are the tactics of the revolutionary class movement. Where two or three revolutionaries use organised violence to attack the class system—there is the Angry Brigade. Revolutionaries all over England are already using the name to publicise their attacks on the system.

No revolution was ever won without violence. Just as the structures and programmes of a new revolutionary society must be incorporated into every organised base at every point in the struggle, so must organised violence accompany every point of the struggle, until, *armed*, the revolutionary working class overthrows the capitalist system.

COMMUNIQUÉ 6

The Angry Brigade.

Communiqué 7 was an even more definitive statement. Politics apart, it was interesting as evidence, in that the writers claimed direct responsibility for the Carr bombs two months earlier and for the Ford bomb, which they said would go off that very evening. It did.

COMRADES!

Two months ago we blew up Carr's house. Revolutionary violence through the high walls of English liberalism. Apart from a short communiqué we remained silent since . . . why? . . . who is the Angry Brigade . . . what are its political objectives . . . a lot of criticism was directed towards vague directions . . . they called us the Special Branch, the Front, Anarcho-Nuts, Commies, Bombmob, the lot . . . we believe the time has come for honest dialogue ... with any comrades who care to address us ... through the underground press ... through anything. Don't look around you brother and sister ... look at the barriers ... don't breathe ... don't love ... don't strike, don't make trouble ... DON'T.

The politicians, the leaders, the rich, the big bosses are in command ... THEY control. WE, THE PEOPLE, SUFFER ... THEY have tried to make us mere functions of a production process. THEY have polluted the world with chemical waste from their factories. THEY shoved garbage from their media down our throats. THEY made us absurd sexual caricatures, all of us, men and women. THEY killed, napalmed, burned us into soap, mutilated us, raped us.

It's gone on for centuries.

Slowly we started understanding the BIG CON. We saw that they had defined our "possibilities". They said: You can demonstrate ... between police lines. You can have sex ... in the normal position as a commodity; commodities are good. You can rally in defence of the T.U.C. .... the T.U.C. "Leadership" is wise.

They used confusing words like "public" or the "national interest". Is the public some kind of "dignified body" which we belong to, only until we go on strike? Why are we reduced then to dreaded scroungers, ruining the country's economy? Is the "National Interest" anything more than THEIR interest?

Lately we started seeing through another kind of con: There is a certain kind of professional who claims to represent us ... MP's, the Communist Party, the Union leaders, the Social Workers, the old-old left. .... All these people presumed to act on our behalf. All these people have certain things in common ... THEY always sell us out ... THEY are all afraid of us ... THEY'LL preach towards keeping the peace ... and we are bored ... poor ... and mainly very tired of keeping the peace.

THE ANGRY BRIGADE BECAME A REALITY when we knew that every moment of badly paid boredom in a production line was a violent crime. We had rejected all the senile hierarchies and ALL the structures, the liars, the poverty pimps, the Carrs, the Jacksons, the Rawlinsons, the Bob Hopes, the Waldrons. .... To believe that OUR struggle could be restricted

to the channels provided to us by the pigs, WAS THE GREATEST
CON. And we started hitting them. January 12th was
important . . . we shattered the blackouts of the Yellow
Press . . . hundreds of years of imperialism . . . millions of
victims of colonialisation were breaking up . . . all the
suppressed frustration, all the glow of unleashed energy was
blowing our minds . . . Carr was totally unimportant . . . he
was just a symbol . . . we could have killed the bastard . . .
or Powell . . . or Davies . . . or any pig.

Then we were scared . . . like any newly born baby opening
our eyes to a gigantic glow—we got frightened . . . every
knock, every word became a menace . . . but simultaneously
we realised that our panic was minute compared to the panic
of the Mirrors and the Habershons AND IT FLASHED: WE
WERE INVINCIBLE . . . because we were everybody. THEY
COULD NOT JAIL US FOR WE DID NOT EXIST. We started daring
out into the open, talking to friends, to neighbours, to people
in the pubs, in football games . . . and we knew that we were
not alone . . . WE WERE ALIVE AND GROWING!

COMRADES!
Brothers and sisters we hardly know have been picked up,
framed, intimidated, harassed. The McCarthys, the
Prescotts, the Purdies are all INNOCENT. The pigs need
scapegoats.

Our power is the 6 Conservative offices petrol bombed on
January 13th, the Altrincham generator which was blown out
are all answers of the Revolutionary Movement to our call.
We are certain that every single day that these comrades
stay behind bars will be avenged. . . . Even if it means that
some of the pigs will lose their lives.

Three weeks ago we nearly blew up Jackson's headquarters. We knew he had to sell out. We wanted to hit him
BEFORE he did the damage. But inside us we carry the
remnants of liberalism and irrationality . . . burdens of our
past we have to shed. He beat us to it. . . . HE SOLD OUT. . . . Let
the working brothers and sisters be our jury.

This time we knew better: it's FORD TONIGHT—we are
celebrating the hundred years of the Paris Commune, we
are celebrating our REVOLUTION which won't be controlled.
Our revolution is autonomous rank and file action—we

create it *ourselves*. We have confidence now . . . we don't have to wait for them to dangle something tempting like a Powell, a Bill, or a bad apple in front of our faces, before we jump like rabbits. We don't clutch desperately at the illusion of FREEDOM. Our strategy is clear: How can we smash the system? How can the people take power?

We must ATTACK, we cannot delegate our desire to take the offensive. Sabotage is a reality . . . getting out of the factory is not the only way to strike . . . stay in and take over. We are against any external structures, whether it's called Carr, Jackson, I.S., C.P. or S.L.L. is irrelevant—they are all one and the same.

WE BELIEVE IN THE AUTONOMOUS WORKING CLASS. WE ARE PART OF IT. AND WE ARE READY TO GIVE OUR LIVES FOR OUR LIBERATION.

POWER TO THE PEOPLE.

COMMUNIQUÉ 7 the Angry Brigade.

This was really the Angry Brigade's political testament, their attempt to explain the kind of libertarian philosophy that they had distilled from marxism, anarchism, situationism, and their own experiences "underground". The debt to Debord was large:

"*They* have tried to make us mere functions of the production process" . . . "*They* made us absurd sexual caricatures . . ." "*They* defined our possibilities" . . .

Then there was the attack on the "recuperators"—the unions, social workers, the "old-old" left, and with a look back to Paris 1968: the rejection of "hierarchies" . . . "the revolution we create ourselves . . . getting out of the factory is not the only way to strike . . . stay in and take over".

As if to emphasise their difference from the orthodox revolutionary groups, on 1 May, the traditional Communist rallying day, they put a bomb in the Biba boutique in Kensington High Street. Again the Spectacular society was the obvious target:

"If you're not busy being born you're busy buying". All the

sales girls in the flash boutiques are made to dress the same and have the same make-up, representing the 1940s. In fashion as in everything else, capitalism can only go backwards— they've got nowhere to go—they're dead. The future is ours.

Life is so boring there's nothing to do except spend all our wages on the latest skirt, or shirt. Brothers and Sisters, what are your real desires? Sit in the drugstore, look distant, empty, bored, drinking some tasteless coffee? or perhaps BLOW IT UP OR BURN IT DOWN. The only thing you can do with modern slavehouses—called boutiques—IS WRECK THEM. You can't reform profit capitalism and inhumanity. Just kick it till it breaks. Revolution

COMMUNIQUÉ 8

The Angry Brigade.

Three weeks after the Biba bomb, there was another "specialised" attack. An attempt was made to blow up the police computer at Tintagel House on the Thames Embankment. Again it was a symbolic gesture against the Spectacular society: Communiqué 9:

We are getting closer.
We are slowly destroying the long tentacles of the oppressive state machine . . .

secret files in the universities
the census at home
social security files
computers
TV
Giro
passports
work permits
insurance cards

Bureaucracy and technology used against the people. . . .

to speed up our work
to slow down our minds and actions
to obliterate the truth.

Police computers cannot tell the truth.

They just record our "crimes". The pig murders go un-
recorded. Stephen McCarthy, Peter Savva, David Owale.
The murder of these brothers is not written on any secret
card.

We will avenge our brothers
If they murder another brother or sister, pig blood will
flow in the streets.

168 explosions last year. Hundreds of threatening telephone
calls to govt. bosses, leaders.

The AB is the man or woman sitting next to you. They have
guns in their pockets and anger in their minds.

We are getting closer.

What interested Habershon particularly about the Tintagel
bomb was the fact that it was timed to coincide with three
attacks on British-owned premises in Paris: a Rolls-Royce
showroom, a British Rail office, and a firm supplying Land-
Rovers. With the bombs was an open letter to Mr Heath,
handprinted in French, protesting at the "repressive tactics"
against revolutionary groups, mentioning particularly the
treatment of Prescott and Purdie.

For Habershon it meant more evidence of the links between
the Angry Brigade and France to add to the French explosives
Yallop and Lidstone had already identified, and the associations
with the First of May Group.

And for the sergeant in the Special Branch who had originally
identified the Situationist influence in the Angry Brigade
communiqués, number 9 was yet more evidence that it was
still strong, if not stronger. On one occasion the same sergeant
notched up a minor triumph during a raid on a flat in Powis
Square, Notting Hill. As he was sifting through some books and
papers he noticed a copy of Debord's *Society of the Spectacle*. He
picked it up. In the margin were some notes, a commentary, as
it turned out, in John Barker's handwriting. Not that it proved
that Barker had anything to do with the communiqués, though
it did show that his political sympathies lay in that area.

A remarkable characteristic of the investigation so far was
that the list of people drawn up as suspects by the Special
Branch through their political inquiries was almost identical to

the list drawn up independently by Habershon through his normal detective inquiries. The reason of course was that so many of the "politicians" were involving themselves in the fraud conspiracy. It was leading one person after another into the net. By now the special fraud team formed to help the Barnet inquiry had discovered that cheque books had been stolen on a grand scale from universities all over the country, but mostly from Oxford, Cambridge and Essex. Cheques from these books had been forged and uttered, and there had also been systematic "cross firing" between accounts to which these stolen books related and Post Office Savings books which had also been stolen on a large scale. The giveaway in all this was the handwriting. Samples from Habershon's suspects were sent to the Police Laboratory at Holborn for comparison with writing on the forged cheques which had been sent from police forces all over Britain. As a result, on 11 June, Prescott, Purdie, Mendelson and three others were charged jointly with conspiracy to defraud. Mendelson did not appear. With Greenfield she had been missing for some time now, and their pictures had been circulated in the *Police Gazette* as wanted persons.

But by the beginning of June, despite some success with fraud inquiries, the position as far as the hunt for the Bombers themselves was concerned was none too happy. True enough, two people were in custody on Angry Brigade charges, but the actual responsibility for the bombing was still a mystery, no matter who Habershon might suspect—and he had about fifteen people he regarded as strong "candidates". He knew several of them had gone to ground, and as he feared, on 22 June, another Angry Brigade bomb went off, this one at the home of Mr William Batty, the chairman in Britain of the Ford Motor Company. At the same time, another bomb went off at an electricity sub-station of the factory itself.

Again there was a communiqué, this one brief:

Brothers and sisters John Dillon's in; we won, Batty and his transformer's out; Put the boot in. Bogside—Clydeside, support the Angry Side. Spread the word. Power to the people. Communiqué 10 the Angry Brigade.

To forestall criticism in the press about the failure of measures to stop the bombs, the Commissioner of the Metropolitan Police,

Sir John Waldron, decided to act. Two days after the Ford bombs, it was announced in the papers that a special "Bomb Squad" was to be formed with headquarters at Scotland Yard. Commander Ernest Bond, then head of the five North London police divisions, would be in charge, with Habershon as his number two. For security reasons, the Yard did not give out Commander Bond's name, so he became known in the press as Commander X, the mystery supremo who had been specially selected to smash the Angry Brigade on orders from the Cabinet itself.

What happened in fact was that the inquiry was simply getting too big and too complicated for the team at Barnet. They, anyway, were largely preoccupied with preparing the case against Purdie and Prescott. The fraud inquiries under Detective Inspector Mould were growing to massive proportions. The Special Branch investigations were also growing, and so, of course, was the forensic side of the case. As each bomb went off it was subjected to the most thorough examination ever undertaken, and now each was examined in relation to its predecessors, and not just scientifically. Other common characteristics, the target, the circumstances, the communiqués, were needed by the scientists for statistics to build an associated set. Some central point of reference was essential, and the Yard was the obvious choice. So Habershon and his team and the thousands of papers and documents that had been accumulating at Barnet were transferred to specially prepared accommodation at New Scotland Yard. The investigating team itself was increased to about forty people. About two-thirds of them were Special Branch officers, the rest, including Habershon, were general duty CID men. The Bomb Squad was born.

CHAPTER SEVEN

Barker, Greenfield, Mendelson and Creek at Amhurst Road

ON 2 JULY, 1971, JUST before lunch, three young people walked into the offices of Lewis & Co., Estate Agents, at 263 High Road, London, N.16. They were looking for a flat, they said, somewhere in the district, not too expensive and if possible self-contained. Mr Lewis looked through his cards. The most likely place to fit their requirements, he suggested, was a two-bedroomed flat at the top of number 359 Amhurst Road, Stoke Newington. It had just become vacant, and the owner, Mr Moses Gross, a wholesale paper merchant, was anxious to find some suitable tenants.

Mr Lewis rang Mr Gross and said that a Mr and Mrs George Buchanan and a friend of theirs, Miss Nancy Pye, were interested in the flat, could they come round to see it. Two days later after a quick look round the Buchanans said they would like to take it. They were issued with a rent book and paid Mr Gross £8·50 for one week's rent in advance, and another £34 as a security deposit. They said it would not be possible to give references just at the moment as they were school teachers, and the term had not finished. Mr Gross was happy enough to let them have the flat at once, and gave them the key.

That afternoon, the Buchanans began to move in. It was not a big job, not a lot to move—a typewriter, books, pamphlets, poster papers, and a dublicating machine they had been using to run off copy for *Strike*. Because, of course, the Buchanans and Pye were Barker, Creek, and Mendelson.

The particular names they were using belonged to people whose cheque books and credit cards they had acquired. It was established practice, if not a necessity, for people living "underground", to use assumed names. Clearly, Barker, Creek, Mendelson and Greenfield had to keep well away from the authorities. For a start, as associates of Purdie and Prescott, the four were high on the list of "those wanted for questioning in connection with . . ." Greenfield and Mendelson were also circulated as "wanted" in the *Police Gazette* for a series of fraud offences, and of course they had jumped bail at Colchester. They had to be careful, discreet. Not that it stopped them seeing their friends, going to parties, moving around various addresses in London. But the people they were mixing with, now, had to be essentially those they could trust. There was no question of the kind of open community activity they had been engaged in for the past eighteen months or so. The political "space" available to them was becoming more limited as the illegalities of their actions grew. In a sense they were becoming professionals, the front-line troops at the sharp end of the class war.

Because of this change in life-style, Amhurst Road could not become a commune in the Grosvenor Avenue sense.

"Things got shared around," said Greenfield, "and people mucked in to pay for food and clothes. We paid the rent together."

A few visitors came and went, but the social side of life in the flat took very much second place to the political work the four began.

One thing they had all felt from the experiences on *Strike* was how difficult it was to get hold of basic information about the way the state operates: how local councils work, who gets the building contracts, and why. They set about finding out, hoping to publish the results and hand them out to Tenants Associations and anyone else who happened to be interested. They started to analyse the Housing Finance Bill, yet another piece of "class legislation", as Greenfield described it: "Someone was going to make a lot of money out of it. I wanted to know who it was that had pressured the bill through Parliament."

Hilary Creek, because of her involvement with the East London squatting campaign, began to interest herself in the private security firms. Were they "alternative" police forces sent in to deal with people like the squatters? Then there was the Situationist interest in urbanism—the way city centres were being redeveloped for profit, and how people who originally lived there were being driven out to make way for middle-class ghettos.

But, of course, the four at Amhurst Road weren't spending all their time thumbing through *Who's Who* and the *Directors' Guide*. All through one night, for example, they were out on the streets of Dalston and Hackney sticking up posters which accused Robert Carr, now Home Secretary, of conspiracy.

Then there was the action round the forthcoming trial of Prescott and Purdie. They had to decide what to do about that. A committee had been set up to organise a rota of prison visits, to provide extra food, letters, literature and anything else that might help. On one thing everyone was determined: the trial must be a *political* trial, not simply the trial of two anti-social, crazy, indoctrinated, red peril, hooligan hippies.

Lawyers were acceptable, but they must co-operate with the defence group, not try to dominate it. The lines of legal battle were already being drawn. First, the defence would concentrate on the way the police had investigated the case. They would call witnesses to demonstrate the "wide range and desperate nature of police raids to look for likely candidates". Then the defence group would stress how the investigation itself had been given top priority, which in turn, gave the police a licence to go to any lengths, even to fabricate evidence. They would draw attention to the way the Special Branch were conducting themselves on "what can we get away with" principles. Detective Inspector Palmer Hall and Detective Chief Inspector Curtis, both from the Special Branch, would be made to take the witness stand. They should use the files of the National Council for Civil Liberties to seek out examples of previous illegal detentions and other abuses of power by the police.

Police witnesseses had to be discredited at all costs, with evidence to show that the law itself was illegal. They should also emphasise the political nature of the Prosecution, the habit of every authoritarian state to use the courts to quell opposition. How could the Director of Public Prosecutions, they would ask, be impartial? They would challenge the principle that the state is always right.

As for the trial itself, there should be no unnecesary restrictions in the public gallery. Police not on special duty should not be allowed in the court. They even suggested who should be called as defence witnesses—anyone who had been threatened or watched by the Special Branch, for example Reg Birch or Vanessa Redgrave.

Barker went to a couple of Defence Committee meetings where that sort of thing was argued out. But he was not too happy about the way it was going. He felt the campaign to free

Prescott and Purdie should be firmly related to a campaign
against police repression in general. Not, though, that there was
any lack of solidarity with Prescott and Purdie at Amhurst
Road. Anna Mendelson put the point strongly.

> When we're nicked we don't leave the rest to pig justice. We
> are not hanging our heads in shame. We're going to work for
> the release of Ian and Jake. We have learnt the strength of
> working together. When we're nicked, we have learned not
> to be intimidated. This is confrontation. We're going to pack
> out the public gallery at Barnet court where we are going
> every time they appear. We're going to shout. We are not
> going to be silent.

Ever since the arrest of Prescott and Purdie the defence group
had made use of the underground press to attack Habershon
and other police involved in the inquiries. In *Oz*, *Frendz*,
Time Out, and in the *International Times*, there was a constant
stream of articles complaining about police behaviour, des-
cribing the raids in graphic detail. At one stage, Habershon was
nominated "Pig of the Year", and there were also personal
and vicious attacks on the Attorney General, Sir Peter
Rawlinson, and on Robert Carr.

Habershon felt strongly that some of this material might add
up, at the very least, to contempt of court. On his raid of
the Agit Prop bookshop, and commune in the flat above, he
seized a large quantity of leaflets and posters of various types
concerned with the defence group's campaign. In Habershon's
view, these articles constituted *prima facie* evidence of a
conspiracy to pervert the course of justice, and he sent them off
to the Director of Public Prosecutions for his consideration. He
also argued that some of the documents were needed for
comparison with and assessment of the Angry Brigade
communiqués. But three of the people living at Agit Prop did
not agree. They applied to the High Court demanding the
return of the material Habershon had taken. They said the
police had no right to seize it in the first place, and no right to
hold it having done so. They argued that the Defence
Committee documents were necessary because they considered
their only hope of justice for Prescott and Purdie rested on a
strong campaign outside the courts. But in his judgement,

Mr Justice Ackner ruled that the material was reasonably held, and that when the police inquiries were completed no doubt the documents would be returned.

Working on Prescott's and Purdie's defence was only a small part of the activities going on at Amhurst Road. The four spent a good deal of time trying to work out their thoughts on paper. They filled exercise books with slogans, draft leaflets, tactics for various campaigns—a right to work campaign, a guaranteed income campaign, a community campaign against "pig" repression. They jotted down reminders—"get quotes from women who've been on strike, talk to women workers to find working conditions, wage relationships".

Time and time again they wrote about the class background of the Industrial Relations Bill.

> Your Boss loves you because you'll take all his shit. Every worker is in the grip of his employer. He is never going to be free or secure while this power relationship exists. The government want total submission.

> Your Boss is your Enemy. You are a function in his concern.

This preoccupation with "class" antagonism characterised the whole libertarian movement. In a letter one man close to the people living at Amhurst Road tried to put across some of the reasons and feelings behind it:

> There is no doubt, no contradiction in the mind of those who keep their country secure for those who rule through money, management, ideas or government, that They are in control, that Their system . . . is basically correct, and that the basis of Their authority, Force, will be used, with the greatest economy, but pursued to the conclusion no matter how inhuman and brutal that end may be. Their power is solely, when it comes to it, the Power to Crush—without remorse, pity or false notions of progress—all opposition. That is how their Fathers got them there, this is how They intend to stay, and this is what they teach their sons. . . . They make the laws for us, not them, to remind us they have total control to exercise any whim, to keep us where we are

by terror, as only they know how—and without any opposition from the friends, the leaders of the oppressed, the
do-gooders, our leaders, the social consciences, because to
waken us up to the war is to risk all their lives, or at least
some more trouble. Trouble they don't like, it mucks up
production and consumer capitalism—and healthy investment a feeling of well being and security inside Their tight
lives. . . . But what about us, the ones they keep down, when
we wake up. There are a lot of roads to take, but only one
deep down that realises our humanity, that gives succour
to hope, for a revenge on everything, every immoral, illegal,
unjust, inhuman, dull, brutish, deadly act, every outrage
against ourselves, our families, our friends, us as individuals
and us as a social group at work, at home, at play, abroad,
everywhere, for a chance to be free to love and create and
try out the possibilities of joy that each one of us knows is
inside us, and that road is resistance. But how can we
resist and hope to win against all this, all their power they
have hundreds of thousands of police, of armed forces, all
the weapons nearly, the dominant ideas at school, in the press,
the T.V. they run most everybody's way of looking at how
life is, they have the resources, the world. They tell us if we
can work, if we are sane and they watch for any resistance.
Do we stand proud and fight them face to face now or do we
wait, do we try and persuade people, but how with so few
resources, do we talk to each other, do we burrow underneath, do we work from within, that is the problem and up to
now most everybody has waited, sold out, pissed against the
wind or battered themselves and each other. But what now?

That last question was being answered plainly enough by the
Angry Brigade. And at Amhurst Road, the whole topic of
violence was constantly on their minds.

They talked about violence as a tactic in the class struggle,
about sabotage. "Do we need to have a perspective on
violence," asked Barker. Someone else tried to define it on
paper:

Extremism is going beyond the point when the guy who's
been exploiting you for years says a joke is a joke, this is
going too far. It's kicking the capitalist when he's down, as he

screams you're not playing the game, when he's never played the game, never in his whole fucking life.

On Saturday, 31 July, an example of that kind of extremism was about to unfold with dramatic clarity. At the flat in Amhurst Road, the duplicator began to run off a communiqué that was an all-out attack on Mr John Davies, the Secretary of State for Trade and Industry.

DAVIES IS A LYING BASTARD
He hides the deliberate rundown of heavy industry, the rundown of investment in the traditionally depressed areas, that's never been much anyway, by saying the closures of UCS are just the result of bad management. And the bloody management won't suffer anyway. The conditions he's made for the new company are tough only for the workers who have to sign a once and for all contract they can't fight according to the Industrial Relations Bill. Davies "courageously" says the government won't support lame ducks. Yet 2 weeks ago the government put a massive investment in Harland and Wolff. A political move to keep capitalism going at any cost in the face of the people's uprising.
    VICTORY TO THE WORKERS ON CLYDESIDE. We'd like to say to you watch out for all the vultures who'll be flying to Clydeside to tell you what to do. The same people who signed the productivity deals that started the redundancy ball rolling are now trying to feed off your struggle. If there's going to be an operation it's got to be for real. Take the yards from the bosses and keep them. The Labour Party, the Unions and their minions, the CP with its productivity craze, the same bastards who always sell us out, will try and fob you off with gestures like one day strikes and one day occupations, petitions etc. which will achieve bugger all.

YOU ARE YOUR OWN LEADERS. HAVE YOUR OWN TACTICS. CONTROL YOUR OWN STRUGGLE—SOLIDARITY. BOGSIDE, CLYDE-SIDE, JOIN THE ANGRY SIDE

COMMUNIQUÉ 11
The Angry Brigade.

As the copies of the communiqué came off the machine, some-

one in the room took out the Angry Brigade stamp, the stamp
that had been used on all the previous communiqués, and
pressed it on to the sheets. The imprint, on three lines, read
Communiqué 11, the Angry Brigade.

Almost exactly at the same time as that little ceremony was
being conducted in cramped, crowded Amhurst Road, across
London in another flat—on the eighth floor of a fashionable
block in Hurlingham, Miss Elisabeth Wilson, housekeeper to
Sir John and Lady Tait, was at home with Sir John and his
nurse, Miss Cummings. Lady Tait was playing bowls at
Hurlingham, and at about ten to five Sir John and Miss
Cummings left to see how she was getting on. Miss Wilson
went out on to the landing to see them off. After they had gone
Miss Wilson turned to go back in again when she noticed a
parcel lying close to the door of the flat opposite.

It was the size and shape of an ordinary shoe box, and it was
done up with pretty gift paper of blue and orange colour
and design, and the parcel was tied with ribbon in the same
colour. On top was a rosette such as one can buy these days
for putting on gift parcels.

Miss Wilson knew that Mr Davies and his wife were away for a
few days, so she went back indoors and rang the deputy head
porter to tell him about the parcel. He was in the bath, so he
told her to ring the hall porter in the porter's lodge and ask him
to come up and get it. She said she would wait upstairs till he
arrived.

I went out of our flat on to the landing, leaving Lady Tait's
front door open. A few moments later as I was standing on the
landing there was a loud explosion. I was dazed and deafened
and discovered that I was bleeding profusely from the leg.

To Habershon, the real target had obviously been Mr Davies,
and he saw the bomb as a dangerous escalation. He ordered
another round of raids, many of them on addresses that had
already be searched several times. But again, nothing. And no
sign either of Greenfield and Mendelson. Then on Sunday,
15 August, there was an explosion at the Territorial Army
Centre in Parkhurst Road, Holloway. Yet more raids, including

one at 90 Talbot Road, the headquarters of the Notting Hill Peoples' Association. In the ground floor front room which was used as a communal coffee bar and meeting place, a detective spotted, pinned to a notice board, an original copy of Communiqué 11, original in the sense that it was stamped with the John Bull printing set, and also an original copy of something called the Angry Brigade Moonlighters Cell communiqué. It was obvious that this last one was designed to go with the TA bomb at Holloway.

COMMUNIQUÉ 12

Over 5,500 refugees, 2,000 homeless, over 20 dead in 2 days, 230 imprisoned without charge or trial, the six occupied counties of Ireland are terrorised by gunmen in khaki. This war of terror is carried out in the name of the British people. THIS IS A SLANDEROUS LIE. The British Imperialist Campaign in Ireland is waged only to safeguard the fat profits of a few rich pigs and power crazy politicians.

We warn all unemployed brothers and sisters.

Do not be fooled by the army recruiting campaign. An army career isn't fun in the sun and learning a useful trade, if you join you'll be trained in Belfast, Derry and all the other working class ghettos in Northern Ireland to murder and brutalize ordinary working class people. That training will come in useful when the boss class sends the troops into Clydeside, Merseyside, Tyneside, Birmingham, London and all the working class districts throughout Britain.

The Moonlighters Cell was a new development, and Habershon asked around to find out what it could mean. The most plausible reason for the use of the name was in memory of a nineteenth-century Irish Patriot/Terrorist who had called himself Captain Moonlight.

Habershon came to two conclusions: first that those responsible for the Angry Brigade bombings were starting a new campaign directed towards and complementing the situation in Northern Ireland; secondly, that as the TA bomb was only two days earlier than their discovery of the communiqué at Talbot Road, there must be a close connection between people using number 90 Talbot Road and the Angry Brigade bombings.

Still the only evidence was association, but although he did not know it Habershon was getting closer.

Towards the end of July and the beginning of August, the four at Amhurst Road were getting deeper and deeper into Angry Brigade activities. The Moonlighters' communiqué was not only run off on their duplicator, parts of it were actually composed by Anna Mendelson, no doubt with plenty of help from the others. The Angry Brigade stamp was kept at the flat. The whole atmosphere was clandestine, exciting. Greenfield had aquired a complete guide to bomb making, and another set of typewritten instructions explaining how to load, fire, strip and maintain a sten gun and a Thompson sub-machine gun. He needed that, because by now they were looking after a sten gun and the 1938 Beretta used against the American Embassy in 1967 and the Spanish Embassy in 1970. How they acquired them, and the ammunition to go with them, remains a secret of the few people involved in the deal. But like the explosives used in all the Angry Brigade attacks, they can only have come from First of May sources.

Barker too was interesting himself in the whole business of armed resistance to the state, and questioning the definitions of legal and illegal actions. He liked to jot down notes to clarify his thoughts on any particular subject. On armed robbery, for example, he wrote that he would need a pistol and a getaway car, and he listed some potential targets—off-licences, late night shops, post offices, with the various advantages and disadvantages. Off-licences for example: there was "little reward, don't know when the money's there, or when the till's cleared". There would be many wasted nights. He even went so far as to keep observation on a post office in Highgate to see when the quiet periods were.

There was a practical reason for these random thoughts on robbery. First, there was a chronic and growing shortage of money at Amhurst Road. The way they were living, collectively and totally committed to the overthrow of existing socio-political order, meant rejection of the work ethic. "If we're conspiring to overthrow the state, we might as well refuse to permit it to exploit half our active lives." Criminality therefore was essential to survival. It was the only way. They had been getting some cash through stolen cheque books and credit cards, but there was no logical reason not to copy the Baader-Meinhoff Group in West Germany, who robbed banks, and try something on a grander scale. Politically it was acceptable, through reasoning as follows:

> Respect for the Law should never be more than a tactical consideration. Legality is a question of power and the Rule of Law is the cornerstone of capitalist domination. It is nothing but a public code defining what society is and how it is to be run. It is enforced on everyone, and where necessary, it is enforced by the physical power of the police courts and prisons. Respect for the Law means respect for the present structure of society. We must get rid of the legality fetish.

But before anyone at Amhurst Road could get involved in anything so dramatic as bank robbery, events were set in train that were to lead, with steady inevitability, to gaol.

CHAPTER EIGHT

The tip-off . . . The raid . . . The arrests

JUST AFTER LUNCH, on 16 August, Hilary Creek left Amhurst Road, as she later put it on record, to see some people in France about an international exchange of the sort of political information they had all been working on for the past few months. At Victoria Station, she drew three pounds in French francs, and with the British Visitor's passport she had applied for three days before, giving, incidentally, a false address, she boarded the train for Paris.

Not long after she had left, as Barker tells it, that same afternoon two people they knew who were involved in Angry Brigade activities came round to the flat. Not unnaturally, the conversation turned to Hilary Creek's trip, and at this point, according to Barker, one of the Angry Brigade took him aside and put a somewhat startling proposition. Would Barker take a message to an Angry Brigade contact in France? A girl would go with him to bring back any replies. But she did not speak any French, so Barker would have to translate for her. The point of the exercise was to work out a plan to help Purdie and Prescott once they had been "sprung" from prison—if, of course, they were convicted; their trial was still a month off. They wanted to arrange places for them to hide on the continent, perhaps on the way to Algeria.

Barker jotted down on paper the substance of the message he was to take to France:

> These are our tactics for the trial. If he gets sent down we'd want to get him out, are you interested? We don't think kidnapping will work. Springing them is one way, the other is a carefully guarded series of actions and threats together. If we did a kidnapping we would also demand the release of, say, someone put in prison for IRB [The Industrial Relations Bill].

The two Angry Brigade people then left the flat, and Barker joined Greenfield and Mendelson for a cup of tea. According to Greenfield, the conversation that followed went like this:

John told me that this bloke wanted him to take a message to somebody in France for him. Anna said, "Hang on. Let's be sure where we stand with this bloke." Because, particularly when I got that lot [the papers about explosives which Greenfield claimed had been left there by the Angry Brigade people] I got the feeling that I was sort of drifting or blundering or being pulled into something I didn't understand, and I don't like being in stuff where I'm not sure where I stand or where I'm going. We three sat down and had a fairly lengthy talk about what our relationship was supposed to be with this bloke, and also about what this message to France was about. . . . John said, "I might as well go anyhow. I've got the message. There's no particular aggravation involved. I'll go and take it anyway."

So, on the morning of Thursday, 19 August, John Barker, alone in his room now that Hilary Creek was away, got up much earlier than usual. He had arranged with his Angry Brigade travelling companion, the girl for whom he was going to translate, that they would go across on the 10:55 boat from Folkestone to Boulogne. It meant that they had to get to Victoria by nine at the latest to get the tickets. And they also had to get twenty-four-hour no-passport excursion cards. That would take a little time, although they both had the photographs required by the form.

The two of them got to Victoria in good time and went straight to the Sealink Travel desk at the side of the station next to Platform One. They got their identity cards first, and then the tickets. The price for two was £8·80. Barker paid for both in cash. He handed over the identification cards. The names and addresses were false, Barker taking the surname Lennox this time; the girl called herself Rosemary Pink. Thus suitably disguised, they made their way to the queue waiting to get on to the platform.

What happened exactly when Barker and "Rosemary Pink" got to Boulogne is in dispute. No one argues about their movements, but over what they were supposed to be doing there, the difference of opinion is acute.

From the evidence they collected, the police have built up their picture of what happened. Hilary Creek, they say, went straight from the Gare du Nord to an address about a hundred yards from the Maubert Mutualité Metro, just off Boulevard Saint Germain. There, they suggested, she met up with a contact from the First of May Group who provided her with thirty-three sticks of gelignite, manufactured the year before at a factory some thirty miles south of Paris, near the village of Cugny.

Barker and "Rosemary Pink" went to Boulogne to meet her so that they could split the consignment between them, and so lessen the risk of capture. It also meant that if anyone did get caught, at least some of the explosives would get through. In fact, the police say, they went through unchecked and arrived back at Amhurst Road near midnight, putting the gelignite in a cupboard under some clothes.

Greenfield was lying in bed awake as Barker and Creek made their way up the stairs and into the flat. He shouted through to them but he didn't bother to get up. Next to him Anna Mendelson, who had been unwell for the past couple of days, was asleep. For all four it was their last night of freedom.

On Wednesday afternoon, 18 August, as Hilary Creek was preparing to leave Paris for London again, Detective Inspector Mould rang through to Commander Bond's office at the bomb squad headquarters at Scotland Yard with some interesting news. He had just heard that Anna Mendelson might be living at an address in North London—359 Amhurst Road, Stoke Newington. Rashly, perhaps, she had been keeping in touch with her family in Stockport through letters. A local "snout", or police informer, had got hold of her London address and passed it on.

Bond asked Mould to see him at his office that evening to talk about it. Habershon went along too, though as he was going on leave the following day he would not be part of any follow up, if there was to be one. By now, the bomb squad's network of informers was pretty comprehensive—some were members of the public acting out of a sense of duty, some were hoping for money, some just tiresome cranks. Bond had to judge the strength of this particular tip-off. Mould was happy with it, and although Mendelson was wanted for fraud only, there was, as Bond pointed out, the possibility of "other matters" entering into the situation. He was thinking of course of Mendelson's and Greenfield's connections with the Angry

Brigade and the bombings. Bond decided to sleep on it, but by the following day, the 19th, he had made up his mind. He called in Mould and told him to mount an operation that would test the value of this information.

Mould's first move was to contact the Special Branch man on the squad to set up observation of the address. The two men chosen to do the job studied photographs of Greenfield and Mendelson, and then just before nine o'clock on Friday morning, the 20th, they drove to Amhurst Road and parked their blue Volkswagen in a churchyard just opposite number 359 to wait.

Inside the flat, Barker and Creek were sleeping off the effects of their trip back from Boulogne. Anna Mendelson was still not well, so it was Greenfield who emerged from the front door first, just before 10:30. He walked along the road a few yards to a telephone box, and disappeared inside. The Special Branch men knew who it was at once. They radioed the news through to Inspector Mould at the Yard. He knew that where Greenfield was, Anna Mendelson was likely to be, too. He told Sergeant Gilham, who had been on the bomb squad since the beginning, to apply for a warrant to search the flat under the Theft Act. Gilham explained to the magistrate that they expected to find stolen cheque books and banking documents. Mould, meantime, got on the phone to Bond to tell him he was going to raid the house, and began to organise his forces.

It was just after four o'clock by the time the police officers involved had gathered at Stoke Newington police station to prepare for the raid. Eight of them were to go in, including a woman police officer to deal with Anna Mendelson, and a uniformed dog-handler with an Alsatian. At just on 4:15 Sergeant Gilham led the way through the front door of number 359 and up the narrow stairs to the second floor. Inside, John Barker was still asleep. Hilary Creek was in the same room, reading. Anna Mendelson was in another room in bed. Jim Greenfield was with her with his shoes off on top of the bed-clothes, also trying to sleep.

Sergeant Gilham tapped on the glass pane in the door. Creek and Greenfield both got up and went into the hall to open the door. Greenfield thought it was the children from next door, but as soon as the catch was undone he knew his mistake. Gilham pushed in, waving his warrant. He was followed by

Sergeant Davies and Detective Constables Doyle and Sivell.
The women police constable stayed outside, in the doorway.

"We're police officers and I have a warrant to search this
flat," said Gilham, according to what he recorded in his
notebook of the conversations that took place that afternoon. It
went like this:

Sergeant Gilham—to Anna Mendelson, lying on the bed,
"What's your name?"

"Nancy Pye."

"I believe you are Anna Mendelson and I'm arresting you
for cheque fraud offences."

It was Constable Sivell's job to arrest Greenfield. He said:
"I believe you are James Greenfield."

"Yes."

"I'm arresting you for a series of cheque frauds and for
burglary."

Anna Mendelson got out of bed. Because of her stomach
ache she could not move very quickly, but within a matter of
minutes she was dressed and on her way downstairs. Greenfield
followed her, a couple of yards behind. Outside in the street
they were put into a green Hillman Minx and driven off to
Albany Street police station, Albany Street because that was
the police station which covered the Euston area, and ever since
the "fraud kit" was found at the left luggage locker, Albany
had been the administrative centre for the fraud inquiries. It
was also from there that the warrants for their arrests had been
issued.

So with Greenfield and Mendelson gone, Gilham and Davies
turned their attention to the flat itself. Barker and Creek were
now sitting together. One policeman noted Barker's flies were
undone. Creek did them up. As Barker wryly put it much later,
when so many of these incidents were in dispute, "the Police
have a spectacularly accurate memory for some things, if not
for others".

But it was a typewriter that first drew Gilham's attention. He
noted the following conversation:

"Who owns the typewriter?"

"Nancy," said Miss Creek.

"And what's your name?"

"Polly."

"Polly what?"

"Just Polly."

Gilham turned to Barker. "And what's your name?"

"Tex."

"Tex what?"

Barker replied, "All right, George Buchanan."

Sergeant Davies meanwhile was looking round the room. Suddenly under a table near the fireplace he spotted what seemed to be the muzzle of a gun sticking out of a blue holdall. Gilham saw it too, almost at the same time, and he pulled the bag out and opened it.

"What are these?" he asked Barker.

"Guns."

"Who do they belong to?"

"They could be anyone's."

"You live here, don't you?"

"Yes, we've lived here for about six weeks."

"Well, where do they come from?"

Hilary Creek replied, "They could have come from any-where."

Next, Gilham noted that he saw some thin metal tubes in a piece of crumpled newspaper on top of a cupboard.

"These look like detonators. Why have you got them?"

"They belong to the Angry Brigade."

And at that point, according to the police, Barker and Creek burst out laughing. Their next discovery, under some clothes in another cupboard, was the gelignite, thirty-three sticks in a plastic bag. Each stick carried the legend: Gommel Antigel Dynamite, *Explosif Rocher, Societé Française des Explosifs, Usine de Cugny*. The date of manufacture was 24 June, 1970.

As Gilham kept his eye on Barker and Creek, Davies went on with the search. He found ammunition clips and some shotgun cartridges in another cupboard on the landing. According to the police, at about this stage, Hilary Creek said she wanted a piss.

"If you must I'll have you taken over to the police station," said Gilham.

"Don't worry," said Creek, "I'll piss in the sink."

She went to the kitchen and closed the door. Within seconds, there was a shout from the policeman who was on the flat roof at the back of the house.

"Look out, she's coming out of the window."

Davies burst open the kitchen door. Creek simply shrugged.
"It was too high anyway."

Not that she would have got particularly far. Two more
policemen were in the garden at the back, one with the
Alsatian.

It was now about five o'clock, and Gilham had to make up his
mind what to do next. He called Davies outside for a moment,
to talk over the situation, and they both agreed that Barker and
Creek should be taken to the nearest police station—Stoke
Newington—as soon as possible. When they got there, Gilham
phoned the Yard and told Commander Bond what had happened. With Mould, he set off at once for Amhurst Road.
Gilham also put a call through to the Metropolitan Police
forensic laboratory at Holborn asking for one of the explosive
experts to come to the flat to deal with the gelignite and
detonators.

In the meantime, with Barker and Creek securely in the cells
at Stoke Newington, Gilham went back to the flat himself to
wait for everyone to arrive. He took advantage of the lull in
events to make up his notes with Sergeant Davies on what had
occurred and been said so far. Bond and Mould, on their way
from the Yard by car, discussed the possible significance of the
find. Privately, Bond was annoyed that he had not gone on the
raid himself.

But the real irony of the situation was that Habershon, the
man who had done more than anyone to try to track the
Angry Brigade down, was not there. He heard the news about
the results of the raid on the BBC's world service in the South
of France where he was touring with his wife. Some of his
colleagues were sure he would head straight for home. But he
did not, and anyway, at that stage, there was little he could have
done. What difference it would have made, though, to the
final outcome if he had been there is still debated by some of the
officers closely involved in the case. His knowledge of the facts
in the inquiry was way beyond anyone else's. Perhaps in that
first interrogation he might have been able to pick up some
points, follow them through, that others missed. As is was he
decided to finish his holiday, read about the case in the papers,
and wait.

By the time Bond and Mould reached the flat—at around a

quarter to six—it was already swarming with police. Men from the fingerprint department were dusting likely areas, a photographer was taking flash pictures of everything that seemed remotely relevant. Captain Hawkins was there from the explosives laboratory, with Sergeant Hopgood to assist him. One of their jobs was to lay out the sticks of gelignite and the detonators for the photographer. Other policemen were looking through the mass of documents in cupboards and drawers. One glance at the scene in front of him and Commander Bond had no doubt in his mind that they had stumbled on the headquarters of the Angry Brigade itself, almost nine months after it had first announced itself to the world.

Bond ordered everything of the slightest evidential value to be taken to Albany police station. A call went to Stoke Newington to transfer Barker and Creek there too. They arrived at about twenty to eight, and after the formalities in the charge room they were put in cells—Barker next to Greenfield, and Creek across a corridor next to Mendelson. Although at that stage they did not see each other, Greenfield and Mendelson must have known that the others had been brought in. The cells are not sound-proof. In fact, one thing the police always listen out for is conversation between prisoners. The object, of course, is to record anything incriminating. In this case, so far, there was nothing. But the night had a long way to go.

At Amhurst Road, by about half-past nine the police searching the place had had enough. They began to pack up the material they had already sorted out. Captain Hawkins put the explosives and the detonators in polythene bags, and took them down to his car. In convoy with some of the other officers, he drove to Albany Street. Bond, who had installed himself in an office on the floor above the charge room, was told of their arrival. Immediately he ordered that everything brought in from Amhurst Road should be laid out on the charge room table, and the four were to be brought out of their cells to see it—separately. He told the officers present to note reactions. This is how they saw it:

Greenfield was brought along from the cells first. According to the policemen who escorted him, his first comment when he saw what was laid out in front of him was, "Yes, fair enough."

He was then asked, "Where did all the explosives come from?"

"Who else have you brought in?"

"I can't tell you that."

"Look," said Greenfield, "I want to tell you everything, but I must have time to think."

"That's all right," said the officer. "Take as much time as you like, but remember we are only interested in the truth. As you know already, you are not obliged to say anything unless you wish to do so and that anything you do say may be given in evidence."

Greenfield replied, "Yes, I realise that, and I'll think about it."

The next person brought from the cells was Barker.

"This is the stuff we've taken from your flat."

"What's Jimmy told you about it?"

"I can't tell you that."

That was all he said, and he was returned to the cells.

Then it was Hilary Creek's turn.

"This is the stuff we've taken from your flat."

Her only comment: "Is that all you've woken me up for?"

Anna Mendelson said simply, "Can I speak to Jimmy?"

This apparently calm, quiet, reasonable attitude on the part of the four when they were confronted with what had been brought back from Amhurst Road was recorded in the notebooks of several officers at the time. It was now somewhere around midnight, and there was obviously a sense among the police throughout Albany station that they were at the centre of some pretty sensational events. The situation was tense. The station itself had become the centre of attention for the hundreds of people who one way or another had become involved in the hunt for the Angry Brigade. It was impossible for the officers on the spot not to feel excited, not to feel a sense of achievement no matter how hardened they were in dealing with criminals, and in some cases that was over many years.

This atmosphere may go some way towards explaining the disparity in the details of what happened at Albany later that night.

Not long after the four had been shown the material in the charge room, two of the officers took two batteries along to Greenfield's cell to ask him about them. They had been found wired together in the holdall with the guns. According to the two policemen the conversation went like this:

"Whose is this handiwork?"

"Mine," Greenfield replied.

"What have you used these batteries for?"

"Nothing. I did it just for fun."

"Have you decided whether you want to tell us anything about the explosives?"

Greenfield said, "It's that gear I'm worried about. Suppose I were to tell you I brought it back from Boulogne yesterday."

At this point the detectives said they had better report the matter to Commander Bond, and left the cell.

The same sequence of events as described by Greenfield went as follows:

As soon as he entered the charge room and saw all the stuff lying on the table, one of the officers pointed out the batteries and said: "This is all down to you, Jimmy, boy." The officer then picked up one of the batteries with some wire attached to it and said:

"What's this?"

Greenfield replied, grinning, "A battery."

"Don't try and be funny with me."

Greenfield said he was then taken back to his cell and beaten up. Hit on the ear, the eye and nose. One man grabbed his testicles and shouted, "I'll screw your bollocks off," while another asked him, "Who was going to France? That was where the jelly's from. If you don't tell us we'll go and do Anna over."

Barker also accused the police of violence that night. He was not taken from his cell to the charge room to see the explosives, he was dragged there by his hair, he said. He said one policeman called him a "fucking long haired shit cunt", and threatened to "bottle" his pretty face through the back of his head.

Whatever the truth was about events at Albany Street that evening, and the various versions are as irreconcilable as the lifestyles of the people who gave them, the situation was the start of the final confrontation with the authorities. The skirmishes over the past months, the raids, the charges and counter-charges, were just the build-up to the clashes to come now that so many people were actually in custody.

Bond, of course, for the authorities, was determined to press home his advantage. The following day, 21 August, he ordered raids on several houses he felt were connected with the people he had arrested. At the same time he told his men to go on with surveillance of 359 Amhurst Road. Early that morning, the

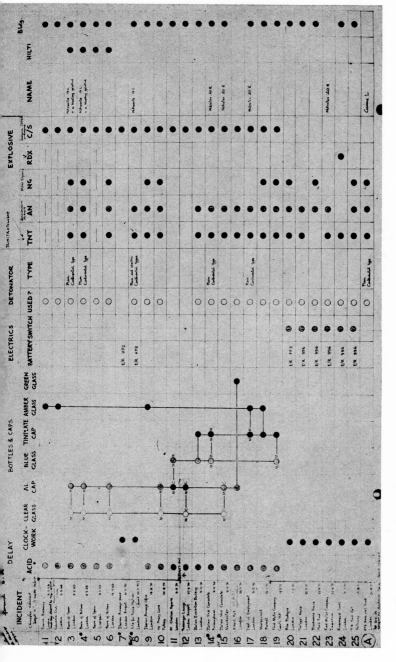

The complex chart drawn up by the Home Office Forensic Laboratory at Woolwich to illustrate the common factors among the twenty-five bombs they claimed were associated in a single set

Ian Purdie, one of the original suspects, hand-handcuffed to a policeman. After spending many months in gaol awaiting trial, Purdie was acquitted

Stuart Christie, another of the original suspects. Like Purdie, he was acquitted after spending many months in gaol awaiting trial

Jack Prescott, sentenced to fifteen years' imprisonment, reduced on appeal to ten

Special Branch men took up their positions again in their blue Volkswagen in the churchyard opposite number 359. But this time one officer was inside the flat itself.

At precisely ten minutes to ten, Stuart Christie walked up to the front door and disappeared inside. He had come round to Amhurst Road "to borrow some money from Hilary Creek", and he was using a car he had borrowed from Albert Meltzer. They more or less shared it on the work they were doing on *The Black Flag*, the monthly anarchist paper they were editing jointly.

Christie made his way up the stairs to the flat. The door was slightly open. He pushed it and shouted, "Anybody there?"

The flat was almost empty, and Christie's first thought was that the bailiffs had been in, and that the four had been evicted, together with their possessions. But as he went into the large bedroom he saw a figure apparently asleep in an armchair. He went across and shook his arm. Just at that point he saw hanging from a nail in the wall a police radio, and he knew what was happening. The policeman woke up with a start.

"Who are you?" he asked.

But before Christie could answer, the Special Branch officer who had been in the car outside, and who had followed him up the stairs, came in behind him.

He said, "I know who you are, don't I?"

In fact, because of his work in Special Branch, this particular detective had known Christie for a couple of years.

After he had been searched, Christie was taken to Stoke Newington police station and handed over to the Station Inspector. An hour or so passed, nothing was happening, so Christie began to kick the cell door, shouting for a solicitor, or if not that, at least a cup of tea. The "Judas Hole" in the cell door opened, and a woman police officer said, "All right then," which calmed Christie down a little. But it was not tea that came into his cell first, it was two police officers. They bundled him out to a car. "No need to be melodramatic," said Christie, as they pushed him into the back seat.

Just as the car was pulling out of the station yard, one of the policemen said, "As you can see, we've brought your car in."

"That car is nothing to do with me. I want to phone my solicitor."

But there was no question of that. He was taken straight to

Albany police station and put into a cell next to the others,

Back at Amhurst Road, the police once more took up their observation posts. About an hour after Christie had been taken out of the house—at about twenty past eleven—Christopher Bott came round the corner into Amhurst Road, and, according to the policeman keeping watch, looked up at the flat, walked by once or twice, and then eventually entered the building. He got the same sort of reception as Stuart Christie, and he was asked the same sort of questions. The police recorded it in their notebooks like this:

"Why did you go round to Amhurst Road?"

"I went to have a drink with John Barker."

"If that's all you were doing," said Sergeant Gilham, "why did you try to run away when you saw the police there?"

"It's not my scene what's going on there."

"What do you mean?"

"You know very well what I mean, dynamite."

"Why do you go there if you don't agree with what they're doing?"

"I knew them all before all this started, I just went to have a drink with John Barker."

By midday there were now six people in Albany Street police station waiting to be questioned in connection with Angry Brigade activities. At 12:35 Greenfield was brought up to the interview room and Commander Bond began his quiet, but firm, interrogation. He began with a caution. Greenfield need not say anything, but if he did it could be used in evidence against him. According to police records, the conversation went as follows—Bond speaks first:

"Last night, you were arrested and brought here and shown property, I propose to ask you some questions about it. All the property was found in your room?"

"It was in the flat."

"You were in bed with Mendelson?"

"Yes."

"In the room you two were in, the guns and gelignite were found, I think that you told one of my officers last night that the gelignite came from France?"

"Yes, that's right."

"Do you want to make a written statement about this?"

"Not yet."

"There were thirty-three sticks of explosives and eleven detonators found in the room, when did they come from France?"

"Thursday, I went there for it."

"Were you alone?"

"Yes."

"Where did you get the explosives, tell me about it?"

Greenfield said, "I was handed two parcels when I got off the boat at Boulogne."

Bond then asked him, "Tell me what happened, did you come straight back?"

"No, I sat around all day."

"Whereabouts in Boulogne?"

"I don't know the names of the roads, but it was just outside the docks, this guy just came up and gave it to me."

"Was it pre-arranged?"

"Yes, a guy told me to go over there."

"Who was it?"

"I don't know."

"Did somebody just come up and ask you to do this?"

"I met him in a pub called The Walford in Stoke Newington."

"Who paid your fare to Boulogne?"

"He did, it was about £7."

"Did he give you any money to pay for the explosives?"

"No."

"Having collected them, where were you to take them?"

"He told me he would come and collect them."

"Having brought them back, where did you take them to?"

"I took them home."

"You mean 359 Amhurst Road?"

"Yes."

"Who was there?"

"Nobody. I just sat and looked at them, there were two newspaper parcels and a little one."

"Tell me, what did this man look like who asked you to do this for him? Describe him."

"A little taller than me, dark hair, not black, not long, not short."

"How old?"

Greenfield didn't reply.

"How was he dressed?"

"I can't remember."

"Would you know him again?"

"Maybe."

"Was there anyone else there when he asked you to do this?"

"No."

"You say there were three parcels, what did you do with them?"

"I put them away without opening them, first of all on the table."

"What time?"

"About half-past eleven on Thursday night."

"When did you open the parcels?"

"Friday morning."

"What time?"

"I don't know, but it was early morning."

"Before 9 a.m. or after?"

"Probably after, but I am not sure, not a long time after."

"Who was there at the time?"

"Nobody."

"Where did you put the explosives then?"

"In a makeshift cupboard by the fireplace."

"Did you know what it was?"

"Yes, that's obvious."

"What did you do about it?"

"I just sat and fretted, the man was coming to collect it on Saturday, that's today."

"So the man knew where to find you?"

"Yes, he knew where I lived."

"Did you open the smaller parcel that you spoke about?"

"Yes, and I found the metal tubes."

"Did you know what they were?"

"Yes, detonators."

"Where did you put them after you opened the parcel?"

"On the table."

"I find what you tell me about this very hard to believe," said Bond.

"Yes, I agree."

Bond went on, "Near where the explosives and detonators were found, that blue holdall was found under the table, you can see what it contains." He showed Greenfield the guns and magazines and the two batteries with the wires attached which there'd been the dispute about the previous evening.

"This bag was in the room that you and the girl Mendelson were sleeping in. What have you got to say about it?"

According to Bond, Greenfield shook his head and looked down to the floor.

"How long have you lived in the flat?"

"About six weeks."

"Who with?"

"Anna and the other two, John and Hilary, that is Barker and Hilary Creek."

"So you have lived there six weeks and you can say nothing about these guns which were found within a few feet of where you sleep?"

Greenfield replied, "I have never seen them before."

"Has anyone ever spoken about them? . . . Who does this holdall belong to? Have you seen that before?"

"I don't know, we all share things."

Bond said, "I don't believe a word you are saying."

The interrogation went on on these lines until about 3:30. Bond went through all the material that Greenfield had been shown the night before in the charge room and he took him through some of the documents. Bond told him that the property he was showing him indicated to him that Greenfield and the others were connected with the Angry Brigade. But as he slowly went over each piece of handwriting for most of the time Greenfield put his head in his hands and looked down at the floor.

After about half an hour Bond finally said:

"Greenfield, we have now spent some time with you going through individual documents and you seem unwilling or unable to give any reasonable explanation about them, so that you can appreciate the seriousness of your position. In fairness to you, I think you must see all these documents found in the flat you were living in with the others. I am now going to spread them out on the table in front of you so that you can look at them and tell me about them if you wish."

Among the material Bond pointed out particularly the typewritten sheets about explosives and sub-machine-guns and how to handle them.

"What about these?"

Greenfield said, "What can I say about them. I seem to be in a real mess."

At about a quarter-past three, Greenfield asked once more to see a solicitor, so Commander Bond broke off the interrogation until he arrived.

Meantime Bond asked that Barker be brought to the interview room. He sat down and immediately Bond began a series of questions about where he was in the flat when the police came in, about whether he knew Hilary Creek, and to all of them Barker simply said, "No reply."

"Why the silence?" said Bond.

"I want to know why I'm being questioned."

"You agree that you were in the flat with Greenfield and the other two?" Barker nodded.

Bond went on, "Myself and other officers have been making inquiries about a group calling themselves the Angry Brigade, and for that reason your flat was searched yesterday. In there was all this property. Do you want to make a statement?"

Barker replied, "I'm not making any statement or signing anything."

Eventually, almost out of a feeling of exasperation, Bond said, "Barker, I have asked you a lot about the documents you see spread out before you on the table. You don't seem to know much about any of this stuff, all of which was found in your flat."

Barker replied, "I have identified the bits that were mine. If I'd known about the other stuff I'd have burnt it. There's nothing I can do about it now. I don't watch what other people do in the flat."

At about 7:15 in the evening it was Stuart Christie's turn to answer the Commander's questions. Bond asked him why he had gone round to the flat that morning.

"I want to see my solicitor," said Christie, and that was his answer to most of the early questioning. Then Bond turned to the car Christie had driven round to Amhurst Road. He told him it had been searched, and produced some plastic bags containing what had been seized. Christie said some of it was Meltzer's and some of it his.

"Show me what's yours and what's Meltzer's."

Christie divided the property out, and Bond went through it all with him. Then, towards the end of the interview after three-quarters of an hour, the Commander produced from under his desk a cardboard box.

"In the boot of your car, police officers found these two detonators. What have you to say about them?"

Christie immediately replied, "I'm saying they were not in the car," and referring to the other things in the car, he said: "I agree with all those, but not with the detonators."

Bond went through some more documents with him, including a letter he said Christie had written which was found in the flat, and then ended the interrogation with a repeat of his first question.

"Why did you go round to Amhurst Road this morning?"

Christie didn't answer.

When he was taken back to the cells, Christie asked for tea.

"We're very busy here," the Station Officer said. Christie replied:

"I'm sure Sir Geoffrey Jackson is getting better treatment in his people's prison in Montevideo."

That same evening Bond, with scarcely a break, went through the same procedure and mostly the same questions with Anna Mendelson and Hilary Creek. They answered by and large with denials and no comments, and with demands to see their solicitors.

For Bond it had been a long session. He had begun at 12:20, and by the time Hilary Creek was back in her cell, it was near eleven o'clock at night. More than ten hours of questioning, and he had got very little out of it. He must have realised already that it wasn't going to be an easy case. He had one more person to see the following morning. Christopher Bott was brought in shortly before midday and immediately said that he had been told by his solicitor not to answer police questions.

"Nevertheless," said Commander Bond, "I'm going to put them to you."

And he went once more through the property brought to Albany Street. To all the questions, Bott made no reply, but when Bond told him he would be detained and charged, he said,

"I would like to say one thing. My solicitor has told me to make no reply, but I would like to say that I have not made any of the bombs."

But by lunchtime on Sunday, Bond had made up his mind that all six people at Albany Street should be charged with conspiracy to cause explosions. The decision to charge them was his, and his alone, based on the evidence found in the flat at Amhurst Road. All six were brought into the charge room, and in the presence of their solicitors, the charges were read out. They were also told to sign for their property. Christie refused to sign the list of goods in his possession while the detonators were on it. After a short consultation with the Station Inspector, Bond signed for the detonators himself. They were cautioned and again each made no reply, each, that is, except for Christie, who simply said, "I am innocent of the charge."

A noted visitor to the police station that Sunday evening was the Commissioner of the Metropolitan Police himself, Sir John Waldron, the man who had had one of the Angry Brigade bombs at his door, and who had personally appointed Bond to take charge of the case.

CHAPTER NINE

*The trial of Prescott and Purdie . . . The committals
. . . The conspiracy indictments*

THE SORT OF thing that had happened at the weekend was
not something that could be kept from the press for very long,
and by the time the Sunday papers were on the streets, they
were full of stories of the dramatic events at Amhurst Road.
Publicly, of course, Bond was still the mysterious Commander
X. And under that name, he let it be known that he had sent out
another wave of detectives on follow-up raids. They called at
addresses in Islington, Holloway, Stoke Newington, Kilburn,
and Notting Hill, but nothing emerged.

On Tuesday, 24 August, four days after the raid, the six
arrested at Amhurst Road appeared at Clerkenwell Magistrates'
Court. At the hearing, Commander Bond, his true identity now
revealed, opposed bail, and they were remanded in custody.
Greenfield and Mendelson, who stood in the dock with their
arms round each other, were further charged that between
12 February and 11 May, 1971, they conspired with Bott,
Purdie, Prescott, Wolf Seeberg, Martin Housden, Peter
Truman, Christine Haisall, Rosemary Fiore, and other
persons unknown "to cheat and defraud such persons who could
be induced to part with money and goods by the use of stolen
cheque books, credit cards and identity documents and other
fraudulent means and devices contrary to common law".

The people on remand were sent to Brixton or Holloway,
and to the shock, if the surprise, of the authorities a new kind
of political consciousness seemed to take root in the prisons.
There was concern about the spread of "subversive" literature.
Leaflets written and printed at a commune in North London
began to circulate the cells at Brixton demanding reforms,
and urging the prisoners to take action if they did not get
them. Suddenly copies of Christie's and Meltzer's book *The
Floodgates of Anarchy* began to appear. Old lags were coming
out of prison and complaining to Habershon about how they
had been approached by these "funny people with their funny

ideas". They did not like it. But among some of the younger prisoners the effect of this influx of libertarian "political prisoners", as they liked to call themselves, was more marked. Their ideas of "resistance", the general discontent that they spread, began to take effect.

From Brixton demonstrations, occupations, even riots, spread to prisons all over Britain in late 1971 and 1972. How much of it was inspired by the presence of the new type of "political" prisoner is difficult to judge. But there is no question that the sort of attitude they brought into prison with them had a profound effect. Greenfield, for example, on one occasion persuaded a fellow prisoner who had been advised by his lawyer to plead guilty, to change his plea and fight his case through. The prisoner did, and was eventually acquitted. As the story spread round, embellished and exaggerated no doubt, Greenfield became something of an anti-Establishment hero figure.

As for Habershon, he had arrived back from his holiday in France on 6 September, the day before the Prescott/Purdie trial was originally due to begin. The date had been fixed long before the discoveries at Amhurst Road and obviously now in the changed situation the police would have liked it altered. They applied to have the two men joined to the Amhurst Road six in the same indictment. To back up their application they put forward evidence that all eight were concerned in the same conspiracy to cause explosions.

By now, of course, Prescott had been in custody for more than six months, Purdie for more than five. To have them wait for the prosection and defence of the six to prepare their cases would have meant keeping them in custody for perhaps a further six months. Obviously the court could not allow that. So, to the disappointment of the police, it was decided to proceed against Prescott and Purdie separately, and the new trial date was set for 10 November.

Habershon, meanwhile, set himself to work on the evidence found at Amhurst Road while he was away. There was a massive pile of documents to go through, letters, leaflets, typewritten drafts of political pamphlets, lists of names and addresses, drawings, plans. Habershon decided to concentrate first on the material that had already been sifted out and identified as having some evidential value. At the same time, he asked the Fingerprint Branch to check back in their records for any marks they had from explosions or attempted explosions that he thought were involved in the conspiracy. If they found any they were to compare them with the fingerprints of the people now in custody.

Habershon knew already that the Branch had some unidentified prints from several bomb incidents, now he wanted them all checked. It was a boring, not to say daunting, task. But it paid off. They identified fingerprints of Greenfield on a newspaper that had been used to prop up the unexploded bomb in a carrier bag on the site of Paddington police station. They also identified marks on papers used to wrap the bomb at the Italian Consulate in Manchester as belonging to Greenfield and Anna Mendelson. Once more, Habershon's persistence had brought results. He pressed on.

In one of the locked property stores in the basement at Scotland Yard lay a huge pile of documentary material seized in the original raid on Amhurst Road, but discarded as having no apparent evidential value. It was almost untouched. Habershon decided to have a look at it himself. He got the key from the sergeant in charge of exhibits, and went down to the vaults. For hours he sifted through every bit of paper until eventually he pulled out twenty-four documents he thought might be of some use in evidence. He sent them off to the handwriting expert at the Holborn forensic laboratory, Mr Ellen, again for comparison with the known handwriting of the people he had in custody, and with the handwriting of some of his other suspects. Later on he had the same documents sent to the fingerprint branch for similar treatment there.

The trial of Prescott and Purdie began on 10 November and lasted almost three weeks. It was, in effect, a curtain raiser, a prologue to the most bitterly contested, most expensive, and by far the longest criminal trial Britain has ever had.

The two men were charged with conspiring between 30 July, 1970, and 7 March, 1971, with James Greenfield, Anna Mendelson, Christopher Bott, James Stuart Christie, Hilary Ann Creek and John Barker, "unlawfully and maliciously to cause explosions likely to endanger life or cause serious injury to property".

Prescott alone was charged specifically with the bomb attacks at the homes of Mr John Davies and Mr Robert Carr.

The main evidence against Prescott came from the two prisoners who had shared his cell at Brixton. Mr A and Mr B said they had heard Prescott boast about his Angry Brigade activities. In particular they said he had talked about taking part, with others, in the Davies bomb attack. To back this up, the Prosecution produced evidence from Amhurst Road of Davies's address and telephone number, along with a list of what they maintained were clearly Angry Brigade targets. But an obvious puzzle for the jury was the fact that Prescott could never have been to Amhurst Road because he was in jail over that whole period. It was a taste of the complexities of the charges in this trial, and the one to come.

More impressive was the evidence of Prescott's handwriting on three envelopes sent out with communiqués after the Carr bomb attack, and then there was the evidence of two girls who had come down from Edinburgh to see Prescott and Purdie, but fled back home because, they said, of all the "revolutionary talk". A good deal was made of the change in Prescott's political attitudes in Albany prison.

"Killing Mr Heath, Mr Maudling and Mr Powell would not be murder," he'd written in a letter to a friend, "the removal of tyrants such as these can only further the cause of humanity."

As for Purdie, he was not only part of the conspiracy, the Prosecution alleged, but one of the key figures behind it. His sympathies were the same as Prescott's.

"We are so much in harmony," he'd once written, "that we become one. And that bodes ill for our enemies."

And that really was about it as far as the Crown's case against Purdie was concerned, that and the fact that he had run away when the police went to arrest him. So thin was the evidence against him that his defence lawyer, Mr Shindler, took the unusual course of persuading his client not to give evidence in his own defence. He took the view that Purdie's lack of involvement ought to be clear enough to the jury. There was nothing to connect him in any way with Amhurst Road, nothing to link him with any of the explosions. The Crown's case against him, said Mr Shindler, was built on an "edifice of suspicion and prejudice".

In his summing up, Mr Justice Melford Stevenson told the jury that "In one sense, politics here don't matter. You may or may not feel a sense of revulsion from a good many of the sentiments read out from these exhibits. If you do, cast it aside. Do not hold it against the defendants."

The only sense in which politics mattered, he said, was where they were relevant to motive for what was alleged to have been done.

"This case is of overwhelming public importance, and it is equally a case of overwhelming importance to the accused."

The Prosecution's allegation, said Mr Justice Stevenson, of conspiracy between a number of people had not been seriously contested. The question the jury had to answer was whether the Crown had satisfied them that Prescott and Purdie, from September, 1970, were parties to that conspiracy.

In the case of Purdie, the jury decided that he was not, and they acquitted him. Prescott, on the other hand, they found guilty of conspiracy, but not guilty of the other charges of causing explosions. For his part in what Mr Justice Melford Stevenson called "the most evil conspiracy I have ever had to deal with", he was sentenced to fifteen years.

"I do not doubt," said the Judge, "that you were chosen as a tool by people more sinister than you are, and I suspect more intelligent. They are as yet unidentified, but I must equally face the fact that you knowingly embraced that conspiracy."

Prescott had pleaded guilty to seven counts on another indictment which charged him with stealing a cheque book, obtaining a railway ticket, clothing, wine and spirits by means of forged cheques. He was given five years for that, to run concurrently.

In mitigation, Prescott's counsel said whoever was responsible for the bomb was far more deserving of punishment than Prescott.

Some day someone may be answerable for the whole scheme. Prescott had a lesser responsibility than others who are not before you today. He is a new recruit to what might be called political violence. The picture emerges of a man much less guilty than many others named or un-named who figured in arranging these outrages.

There is no question that the severity of the sentence on Prescott was a shock, not only to those in his own circle, but to many people outside it. "Fifteen years for addressing three envelopes", was how some of his supporters saw it. Others felt that it was only to be expected from the Judge who had presided at the Garden House trial, and who had imposed such heavy sentences on the students on that occasion.

The *Guardian* said the fifteen-year sentence seemed "exceedingly severe". It questioned whether Prescott was really the right man to suffer an exemplary sentence. "His opinions (as distinct from his actions) are the understandable products of a wretched life." The whole trial, said the paper, had been "an unsatisfactory affair". The main charge, that Prescott had taken part in the Carr bomb attack, had failed. Purdie was acquitted, and Prescott convicted on the much vaguer charge of conspiracy by a jury which seemed, to judge from the length of their deliberations, to have been much puzzled. The situation was left even more obscure by the decision to proceed later against others alleged to have been in the same conspiracy.

The police themselves certainly believe that, had there been just one trial, the result might well have been very different.

Largely as a result of Habershon's persistence four more names were eventually added to the conspiracy charge. On 11 November, the day after the start of the Prescott/Purdie trial, Angela Weir, a twenty-seven-year-old teacher, was arrested at an address in North London. She was taken to Albany Street police station and confronted by Bond.

"I still can't understand why I have been brought here. It's nonsense."

She said she had never been to Amhurst Road, she had never heard of any of the people living there, nor did she know personally Purdie or Prescott.

"Then why was your name and telephone number in Prescott's address book?" said Bond.

There was no reply. When she was shown the guns and explosives from the flat, she said she had never seen them before.

"It's fantastic where they get this stuff from."

Bond suggested that it was she who'd gone to France with Barker to collect the gelignite.

She said, "I don't know what you're talking about. You will have to prove every bit of it."

A week later, Chris Allen, a play leader in Notting Hill, was arrested, and with a university lecturer, Pauline Conroy, taken to Albany Street. Both were added to the list of alleged conspirators. Then on 18 December, Kate McLean, a twenty-one-year-old art student living at Grosvenor Avenue, was taken into custody, making a total now of ten on the indictment list.

The committal proceedings opened at Lambeth Magistrates' Court on 3 January, 1972. The Prosecution began by saying that the Attorney General was not granting his *fiat* for proceedings to continue against Allen and Conroy, so they were dismissed from the case. Miss Conroy was given £150 costs, and her property was restored to her. Allen was given £100 costs, and his belongings were returned.

The hearing at Lambeth lasted for three weeks before the eight left on the indictment were committed for trial at the Central Criminal Court. The charges against them were lengthy and specific:

Regina *v.* James GREENFIELD
          Anna MENDELSON
          George BUCHANAN, alias John BARKER
          Hilary Anne CREEK
          James Stuart CHRISTIE
          Christopher Michael G. BOTT
          Angela Margaret WEIR
          Catherine Judith McLEAN

For that they on divers days between 1st January, 1968, and 20th August, 1971, in the Greater London Area and elsewhere, unlawfully and maliciously conspired together with Jack PRESCOTT and with persons unknown to cause by explosive substances explosions in the Unived Kingdom of a nature likely to endanger life or cause serious injury to property.
Contrary to Section 3 (a) Explosive Substances Act, 1883

James GREENFIELD and Anna MENDELSON.
On or about 9th October, 1970, at 26 Brown Street in the City of Manchester, unlawfully and maliciously attempted to cause by explosive substances an explosion in the United Kingdom of a nature likely to endanger life or to cause serious injury to property.
Contrary to Section 3 (a) Explosive Substances Act, 1883

*Christopher BOTT, John BARKER, James GREENFIELD,
James CHRISTIE, Hilary CREEK and Anna MENDELSON.*
On or about 20th August, 1971, at 359 Amhurst Road,
London, N16, knowingly had in their possession or under
their control certain explosive substances, namely, thirty-
three $3\frac{1}{2}$ oz. cartridges of explosive; eleven detonators; one
cardboard box lid containing a plastic container with six
Jetex charges therein; a tinplate lid; an electrical light switch
cover and screw; two lengths of conductor wire; one length of
lay flat flex; one 2·5v. bulb; one 1·5v. dry battery; one used
tube of Bostik adhesive; three resistance panels; one piece of
emery cloth; one pin; one polythene bag containing one
length of nichrome wire; one length of white cotton string;
one resistance element; one ruler scale; two PP3 9v. batteries
connected in series; one part-used tube of Bostik adhesive;
one pair of black leather gloves; one pair of black fabric
gloves; one blue/grey holdall: in such circumstances as to
give rise to a reasonable suspicion that they did not have them
in their possession or under their control for a lawful object.
Contrary to Section 4 (1) Explosive Substances Act, 1883

John BARKER, James GREENFIELD and Hilary CREEK.
On or about 20th August, 1971, at Walford Road, London,
N. 16, knowingly had in their possession or under their
control certain explosive substances, namely a roll of $\frac{1}{2}''$ black
insulating tape and a pair of scissors, in such circumstances
as to give rise to a reasonable suspicion that they did not have
them in their possession or under their control for a lawful
object.
Contrary to Section 4 (1) Explosive Substances Act, 1883

James CHRISTIE.
On or about 20th August, 1971, at Sydner Road, London,
N. 16, knowingly had in his possession or under his control
certain explosive substances, namely, two detonators and a
screwdriver, in such circumstances as to give rise to a reasonable suspicion that he did not have them in his possession or
under his control for a lawful object.
Contrary to Section 4 (1) Explosive Substances Act, 1883

James CHRISTIE.
On or about 10th June, 1970, at 16 Fonthill Road, Finsbury

Park, London, N4, had in his possession a round of 7·65mm ammunition without holding a Firearms Certificate in force at the time.
Contrary to Section 1 (1) Firearms Act, 1968

James GREENFIELD, John BARKER and Hilary CREEK.
Between 8th July, 1971, and 20th August, 1971, in the Greater London Area, dishonestly handled a Hillman Avenger motor car, FGJ505J, knowing or believing the same to have been stolen.
Contrary to Section 22 (1) Theft Act, 1968

Christopher BOTT, John BARKER, James GREENFIELD, James CHRISTIE, Hilary CREEK and Anna MENDELSON.
On or about 20th August, 1971, at 359 Amhurst Road, London, N. 16, had in their possession a Browning 7·65mm pistol without holding a Firearms Certificate in force at the time.
Contrary to Section 1 (1) Firearms Act, 1968

Christopher BOTT, John BARKER, James CHRISTIE, James GREENFIELD, Hilary CREEK and Anna MENDELSON.
On or about 20th August, 1971, at 359 Amhurst Road, London, N16, had in their possession 81 rounds of ammunition without holding a Firearms Certificate in force at the time.
Contrary to Section 1 (1) (b) Firearms Act, 1968

Christopher BOTT, John BARKER, James GREENFIELD, James CHRISTIE, Hilary CREEK and Anna MENDELSON.
On or about 20th August, 1971, at 359 Amhurst Road, London, N. 16, had in their possession without the authority of the Secretary of State, prohibited weapons, namely, a Sten gun, a sub-machine gun and a Beretta sub-machine gun.
Contrary to Section 5 (1) (a) Firearms Act, 1968

James GREENFIELD.
On or before the 22nd May, 1970, at Harrow Road, London, W2, unlawfully and maliciously attempted to cause by explosive substances an explosion in the United Kingdom of a nature likely to endanger life or cause serious injury to property.
Contrary to Section 3 (a) Explosive Substances Act, 1883

Those, then, were the charges, read out and their nature explained in ordinary language. Each was asked if he or she wished to answer to them, and if so:

You need not say anything unless you wish to do so, and you have nothing to hope from any promise, and nothing to fear from any threat, that may have been held out to induce you to make any admission or confession of guilt. Anything you say will be taken down and may be given in evidence at your trial.

Barker began the replies with a carefully prepared statement:

It's become clear from the Prescott/Purdie trial, and from these proceedings that we are not going to get a fair trial.

At the trial of Ian Purdie and Jake Prescott, six of us here were tried in our absence, and assumed to be guilty throughout. This also meant that Jake was largely found guilty on the basis of his association with some of us—based on *allegations* about what we were and what we did.

All these allegations were accepted *as fact* by the judge, and used in this way in his summing-up. They were also produced as fact in all newspapers at the time. Any jury we will get will have read those reports.

The summing-up in that trial was simply a repeat of the prosecution and a put-down of the defence and included a definition of conspiracy so nebulous that I can't see why the police are trying, grafting in this court so hard for a conviction by any means. Melford Stevenson has done all the work for them.

There is one point in the summing-up of that trial—which was our trial as well—which I want to mention, that is the warning from the judge to the jury—"if you do not believe Mr A and Mr B (two prosecution witnesses) you must come to the conclusion that there was an evil conspiracy between Mr A, Mr B and Mr Habershon". Well, the jury didn't believe Mr A and Mr B; if they had Jake Prescott would have been found guilty of *actually* causing two explosions. Well, where does that leave Habershon? It leaves him strategically seated in this court protecting *his* interests, directing the show. A show that's been like a bedroom farce with witnesses disappearing through doors at breaks in their evidence, and Mr Habershon chasing them through the door. The defence has protested only once of this, probably too late.

Several defence applications to see important documents used in evidence against us or relevant to us have been refused with excuses like "the public interest". What this euphemism boils down to is that "the public interest" in this court is synonymous with the interests of the police.

And the police in this case as in many other cases are committed to getting a conviction by any means possible. The production of extra witnesses to back up other witnesses whose evidence has been a tissue of half truths and untruths, the withholding of documents, and documents from our flat which are not consistent with this conspiracy charge and in fact contradict it, and above all the refusal of bail, throughout the last 5 months.

All on the grounds that we would continue the conspiracy. How I was supposed to do that from Berwick-on-Tweed was never revealed by Commander Bond, perhaps he believes I have a radio transmitter to all the world's anarchists who Habershon produced out of his magic hat the other day, I don't know. He didn't explain. He wasn't required to.

The real reason we're not getting bail is because of what we are, what we believe, not any crime we're alleged to have committed. When it comes down to it the cops just have to say we're anarchists, and it's no bail, or as it used to be—these people live in communes. Me, I'M not an anarchist, but what the cops are getting at is a way of life and thought they don't like. And if they don't like it—well, it's in the public interest to put them away.

Being on remand in custody is a penalty. Whether consciously or not it prevents us really getting our defence together. We're separated, can't contact defence witnesses, have a hard time getting joint conferences together. During this committal we get about 2 minutes of fresh air per day. Both the magistrate and Bond have said what happens in prison is nothing to do with them. Well, it is. It's you (the magistrate) who ensures we return there. And you our magistrate are *irresponsible* when you say that it's not your affair that my sisters can't prepare their defence without it being read.

There is a conspiracy in this court. A conspiracy to get a conviction by any means. And one of the means is to ensure it is as difficult to prepare as possible. You, Mr Magistrate, are acquiescent towards this conspiracy.

Barker's statement to the Lambeth Magistrate contained the warning shots in the coming confrontation. The words "Whose Conspiracy?" which ended up as graffiti on the walls of the Old Bailey itself, summed up the way the defence was going to be played. But how to get it together was a problem, and a constant complaint by the defendants, some of whom were already planning to act on their own behalf throughout the coming proceedings. Anna Mendelson expressed her dismay in her statement to the magistrate.

Both Hilary and I have been in Holloway for over 5 months. The prison system is geared to sap your energy and creativity. To ask you, the Magistrate, to conceive of the isolation and repression, both physical and mental, which people are subjected to in these places is, I'm sure, asking too much, for you have never experienced nor are you ever likely to experience a gaol sentence, and although the lawbook states that we are innocent until proven guilty, we are in effect serving a sentence right now. This is the time when we should be preparing our defence as we wish but what happens? We have access to *nothing*, no library, no confidential paper, a promise from the Home Office that joint conference with our co-defendants will be stopped—2 people in a 10 by 7 cell with $\frac{1}{2}$ hour's exercise a day and under *THESE* conditions we have to struggle for our basic right: to defend ourselves at trial.

Greenfield's statement took much the same line:

I endorse what my friends have said and also to make a protest against the total hypocrisy present in a state of affairs when on the one hand people can say that it is not the function of one part of a state to interfere in the affairs of another. This is a lie. Since on Friday the Governor of Brixton Prison had made an attempt to get Buchanan and myself placed in the same cell so that we could go some way towards adequately preparing a defence. The fact that we are still not together comes not from any act on the part of the prison but purely because they have been ordered by Commander Bond to keep us totally separate. Commander Bond had a very definite interest in making sure that we do not coherently counter the charges made at our door. Since he is the head of a Squad of Secret Police who must get results.

CHAPTER TEN

The Court drama begins . . . Jury selection . . .
The "McKenzie" helpers . . . The Prosecution
opening

THE TRIAL PROPER began in Court Number One at
the Central Criminal Court, the Old Bailey, on 30 May, 1972,
before Mr Justice James. From the beginning, it was clear that
the libertarian challenge to the right of the ruling class to rule
was to be brought into the court proceedings as well. Anna
Mendelson, supported by John Barker, applied to the judge to
have the trial postponed for two years. She argued that a "fair"
trial was clearly not possible because of all the publicity about
the case in the press. Obviously the jury would be influenced by
the sensational nature of the reporting. She produced a sheaf
of press cuttings to back up her application. But the judge
would have none of it. What he did allow the defence to do,
however, was to put a list of questions to potential jurors, a
more elaborate list than ever before in a British court.

Nine questions were put by the defence. They ranged from
whether a potential juror was a member of the Conservative
Party, did they have relatives serving with the Army in
Northern Ireland, were they associated in any way with people
or organisations that were Angry Brigade targets, to whether
they felt they would be biased against the defendants because of
their "anarchist" views. Potential jurors were also reminded
that if for any reason they felt that they could not give the
accused a fair trial, they should say so and they would be
excused.

As a result of the questioning, seventeen possible jurors were
ruled out because they said they would be biased, another
thirty-seven were challenged by defence questioning, and two
were challenged by the Crown. In the end the defence got the
kind of jury they wanted. They were already determined that the
trial was going to be a political trial, so obviously a jury who
would be sympathetic to their political views was crucial. They
wanted to eliminate, therefore, anyone with a "bourgeois"

background. They wanted twelve people from the working class. This way, they felt, the jury, as people already oppressed by the system, would understand their position more readily. They also felt they could relate and identify with a working class jury more effectively than a middle class one who would have a built-in prejudice and therefore antagonism. As it turned out, the jury that was finally selected was broadly working class. In fact, five of them had been living on Social Security, "Claimants" themselves, much to the disquiet of the police in the case.

It was plain by the end of the first day that this was going to be no ordinary trial. Among the police who had been involved in the growing confrontation with the libertarians over the past few months there was surprise and not a little resentment over the Judge's latitude in the selection of the jury. Mr Justice James may not have realised it yet, but they, at least, were aware that everything that could be challenged in a court of law was about to be challenged. The defendants would certainly not accept the evidence of people paid by the state whose very existence they were against. They would argue that every word the prosecution witnesses came out with would be governed by their class aspirations. So every word the police, for example, offered would be challenged, and so would their integrity. After all, the eight had nothing to lose, and by accepting the rules of the court, by making any kind of admission, concession, they would be consenting to, accepting, everything they despised.

As justification they could also cite, and did, a paragraph from Brigadier Kitson's book *Low Intensity Operations*. He argued that any nation preparing to defend itself in the late seventies must be as well prepared to handle subversion and insurgency as to take part in orthodox military operations: The Law, he wrote,

> should be used as just another weapon in the Government's arsenal, and in this case it becomes little more than a propaganda cover for the disposal of unwanted members of the public. For this to happen efficiently, the activities of the legal service have to be tied into the war effort in as discreet a way as possible. . . .

The group about to go on trial believed that what Kitson

was saying had already come to pass. Therefore they had to draw up their tactics to fight their "disposal" as "unwanted members of the public". This letter was found at Amhurst Road:

> We must see the court as a place like all others where we act collectively and politically. Their machinery is only of any importance as a weapon of intimidation, trying to isolate us. We are together. We cannot be isolated. There is no such thing as a political trial, all trials are political trials. We are not in court to beg forgiveness for our guilt. There is no guilt. Guilt and innocence are Their concepts, not ours. So you've got a legal aid solicitor, if they deign to give you one. He probably doesn't give a fuck about you. He gets paid the same no matter what the verdict is. We don't want disinterested fools begging and pleading for us in front of this charade. Collective attacks on the court involve challenging the rights of the court to try us, challenging the idea of individual guilt or innocence, bourgeois truth. It needs to be done collectively so we don't need "experts".

It was in this atmosphere that Mr John Mathew, on behalf of the Crown, rose to his feet to begin the case for the prosecution.

> Members of the jury, he began, would you look at the charge sheet. You will see at the top of the first page "the Queen against . . ." and then you will see the names of the defendants.

Mr Mathew proceeded to introduce each of them to the jury. The eight sat in two rows in the dock—the four from Amhurst Road in the front, the others in the back. "The first of the defendants," Mr Mathew began,

> is James Greenfield. He's sitting in the front row furthest from you in the dock, in the red shirt—and he is represented by Mr McDonald and Mr Tansey. Now the next three defendants—Anna Mendelson, in green, and next to her, John Barker, and then Hilary Anne Creek.
> Members of the jury, those three defendants are representing themselves. That's something they do of their own choice

in this case. They have a solicitor to help them, but he has, of course, no right of audience in this court, and therefore as far as this court is concerned they are representing themselves.

But the three were certainly not without support in court. They had round them what have become known as "McKenzie" helpers. As an alternative to legal aid, from the case McKenzie v. McKenzie in 1970, the Court of Appeal held that any person, whether he was professionally qualified or not, could attend a trial as a friend of the defendant to take notes, quietly make suggestions, and give advice. Since that ruling the use of "McKenziemen" and women had been growing slowly, mostly in drug cases at a magistrates' court level. But at this trial they really came into their own. One McKenzie helper went so far as to join the defence solicitors as a Clerk. He was in on all the meetings held to formulate the defence.

The advantage of McKenzie help, apart from the obvious political gestures involved—self-help, self-management in practice—was above all its flexibility in court. The helpers were not tied to the formalities and practices of the Bar. They could "bend" the rules. It was also reassuring for the defendants to have their friends around them, people who sympathised with them genuinely, who really cared about the proceedings, and who had often had the same sort of experience with the authorities themselves.

The McKenzie people, with their jeans and long hair, added to the atmosphere of dissent, and in the austere formality of the Central Criminal Court they were a bizarre contrast to the smart-suited, clean-cut barristers and young men from the Special Branch who sat around outside the court room.

Mathew turned to the second row of the dock. There was Stuart Christie at the end, with his long black hair looking like some latter-day Cavalier; then Christopher Bott, pale and drawn with long fair hair. Next to him were the two remaining girls, Kate McLean and Angela Weir.

"Now, members of the jury, it is my task to tell you what this case is all about," said Mathew.

The allegation in this case is that these eight defendants, calling themselves revolutionaries and anarchists, under various names, sought to disrupt and attack the democratic society of this country with whose structure and politics they apparently disagree. To disrupt it by a wave of violent attacks over quite a lengthy period; that is, by causing explosions aimed at the property of those whom they considered to be their political or social opponents.

Mr Mathew then outlined various bomb and machine gun attacks going back to the Grosvenor Square shooting of 20 August, 1967. He said it was the Crown's case that they were all linked:

in that they had so many common factors that they are all clearly associated, and therefore the responsibility for them can be shown to emanate from a common source. All the defendants, it is alleged, were part or parties to that common source. It may well be that a number of persons other than these defendants were involved in one or other, or more, of these incidents, and a man called Prescott was certainly one of those other persons who were involved, but it is specifically alleged, and the Crown will seek to prove, that anyway over part of this period of three years, during which these serious explosions took place, these defendants were parties to this conspiracy of violence, although it is not alleged that necessarily all of them were parties over the whole period.

What Mathew was saying in effect was (and perhaps the jury might be forgiven for not grasping the complexity of it immediately), that to make the conspiracy charge stick, the Crown did not have to prove that the defendants were involved with all the bombs the Crown said were linked. Nor was it necessary for the Prosecution to show that the eight always acted as a group. It would be enough to prove that any one of them had something to do with any one of the bombs to make out the conspiracy case against him.

The ten remaining charges were somewhat easier to explain. Greenfield only was charged with an attempt to cause an explosion at the site of Paddington police station, because his fingerprints, it was alleged, were found on the wrapping of the bomb. Greenfield and Mendelson were charged with an attempt to cause an explosion at the Italian Vice-Consulate in Manchester. Again fingerprints was the evidence offered.

Christie alone was charged with possessing a round of ammunition. The charge of possessing explosives applied to the first six defendants, those associated with the Amhurst Road raid. So were charges of possessing firearms. Again only Christie was charged with possessing explosives—the detonators found in his car.

As far as possession was concerned, the indictment read that the defendants had these things "in such circumstances as to give rise to a reasonable suspicion that they did not have them in their possession, or under their control, for a lawful object". It was for the defendants to show, said Mathew, that if they did have them in their possession, it was for a lawful object.

But it was the overall conspiracy charge that the trial was really to be about. Two of the defendants—Bott and Weir—were there because of that charge alone. Mathew explained to the jury how he hoped to prove it. He said he would divide his case into three compartments.

First of all, he would have to prove the details of each one of the twenty-five explosions involved in the conspiracy, and the details of the two shootings. Forensic witnesses would say that in their view they were all linked, with each other and also with the explosives, detonators, and other material found at Amhurst Road. That would be the first part of the case— proving the links between the bombs themselves and the material found at the flat.

Then the second part of the case was the arrival of the police on 20 August at Amhurst Road, what they found there and, in particular, the significance of the documentary material.

Finally, there was the interrogation of each of the defendants. That was the police evidence, though as Mathew pointed out, as far as the Crown was concerned, "one can almost summarise the whole of that evidence in a sentence or two by saying that these defendants largely made no admissions or indeed made no denials, having refused to reply".

So there were the three principal blocks of evidence in the Crown's case: first the associated set of bombings, second the material found at Amhurst Road, third the defendants themselves and what they had said.

To prove the conspiracy, Mathew had to convince the jury that the bombs were an associated set, and then that the set emanated from a common source—the eight. In other words, he had to provide the scientific evidence to make the set stand, and once having done that he hoped to link the defendants to the set through the material found at Amhurst Road. It was a daunting prospect, even for a man of Mathew's experience in the courts. But as simply and explicitly as he could he began to outline for the jury the way the Crown proposed to tackle the case.

First the scientific evidence: just how were the twenty-five bombs in the set linked. Mr Yallop would be the principal witness here, with his assistant Mr Lidstone, who had done most of the groundwork and correlation. They would explain how they had arrived at the twenty-five particular bombs in the set from the thousand or so cases that had gone through their hands at Woolwich over the past four years.

Basically the bombs in the set that finally emerged were of two distinct types, different because of the way they were exploded. The first group had an acid delay system. Sulphuric acid in a small bottle burnt its way through a paper membrane in the neck and dripped through holes in the cap on to a mixture of sugar and potassium chlorate. This led to an immensely hot sheet of flame which set off a detonator embedded in the explosive. Seventeen of the bombs in the set had this method of starting the explosion. Six of the remainder were time bombs. "They worked like this," said Mathew,

> instead of acid eating its way through a piece of paper you used a clock. When one of the hands reached a certain point on the clock face it touched a wire which led to a battery. This put a current through the detonator which then set off the explosive.

In Mr Yallop's opinion, there was absolute similarity between the groups through their chemical links. For example, some of the acid delay bombs had the kind of explosives used in some of the time bombs, and vice versa. But as well as similarities in the explosives used, there were many other factors common to both groups. Detonators, for example, then the type of equipment and the technique used to make up the bombs, and of course there were the Angry Brigade communiqués which linked ten of the bombs in the set together. All this would be offered to the jury as evidence that the twenty-five bombs stretching over three and a half years were linked by so many characteristics that they did indeed make up one set.

Mathew next had to convince them that the eight on trial were in some way responsible for that set, and therefore guilty of the conspiracy. He took the bombs in order, pointing out in what ways any of the defendants were related to them. He began with those in the set claimed by the First of May Group. In fact he went further back—to the machine gun used by the group to fire eight bullets at the American Embassy in Grosvenor Square on 20 August, 1967. The gun used in that attack—a 38 Beretta—it would be proved, was found almost exactly four years later at Amhurst Road. As for the First of May bombs, Mathew drew attention to their similarity in make-up, and pointed out that two men, arrested after one attack with a First of May communiqué in their pockets, lived at the same address as the defendant Stuart Christie, though Mathew stressed that there was nothing to connect Christie with the bombs themselves. He had denied having anything to do with the matter at all.

Next Mathew asked the jury to note the similarity between the First of May bomb on the plane at Heathrow and the one found a week later on the site of the new Paddington police station. Both were time bombs, and both had gas element igniters of a type then being used by the firm William Press to convert gas fires. "And," said Mathew, pausing only slightly to let the significance sink in, "members of the jury, you might find this very important in this case, at that very time the defendant Stuart Christie was employed by William Press to carry out that type of gas appliance conversion."

Mathew's task was to try to connect Christie to the First of May Group as firmly as possible. He drew the jury's attention to some imitation American dollar bills the police had found in Christie's flat. They were overprinted with the words "First of May Group".

"The strength of that," Mathew said, "will be for you to decide."

Again with regard to the Paddington bomb, Mathew said that on the bag used to carry it to the site, and on a copy of the *Evening Standard* used to keep the bomb in position, were Greenfield's fingerprints.

The next bomb in the set with evidence linking one of the

eight was at Sir John Waldron's house in Roehampton. An expert would say that the two letters written after the bomb were in Kate McLean's handwriting. "A small, but nevertheless important, part in this matter," as Mathew put it.

Next the three Italian bombs, how did they fit in? They were all on 9 October, 1970. They were similar in make-up, and the communiqués sent with them were all in the name of the Italian anarchist, Giuseppe Pinelli. Mathew said Greenfield's fingerprints were found on the envelope that contained the workings of one of the bombs, and Anna Mendelson's fingerprints were on a magazine at the bottom of the bag that contained the whole device. There was also some evidence, "again the weight will be for you to decide", to connect Christie with the man Pinelli. His telephone number was found in Christie's address book.

Mathew turned to the last group of bombs in the set—those actually claimed by the Angry Brigade itself. He had tried to show through the American Embassy machine gun attack the link between the First of May Group and Amhurst Road, where the Beretta was found. Now, with the shooting at the Spanish Embassy at the beginning of December, 1970, he was to get a link between the First of May Group, Amhurst Road and the Angry Brigade itself. A bullet recovered from the Spanish Embassy, Mathew said, was fired from the Beretta that was used on the American Embassy two years previously. At the same time, after the Spanish shooting, the *International Times* received a communiqué claiming responsibility for the Spanish Embassy shooting. It was signed "The Angry Brigade". This was the direct link between the First of May Group and the Angry Brigade that the prosecution was anxious for the jury to understand. It was the linchpin of the whole associated set as presented by the prosecution, and Mathew went over the circumstances in some detail before going on.

With each bomb, he read out the communiqué that followed it, or the parts at least that he felt were relevant. When he had completed his description of the twenty-five bombs which the Crown said were one set, and when he had outlined the evidence there was to link any of the defendants directly to the bombs at the time they had gone off, Mathew turned to his second block of evidence for the conspiracy charge—the material found after the raid on Amhurst Road.

The flat, said Mathew, was clearly a factory for the manu-facture of bombs. It was also an arsenal of guns and explosives, with documents which suggested that plans were in hand for bombing the houses of prominent people. If the jury believed this, and if Mathew could establish that the defendants were responsible for the bomb-making equipment, that it was "theirs", and then if he could show that the bombs they were making fitted into the pattern of the bombs in the set, he could, as it were, "cement" the defendants into the whole set and so prove the conspiracy.

He then took the jury through the list of exhibits found at Amhurst Road in some detail, pointing out again how they were linked with the defendants. Two rounds of ammunition found there were identical to a bullet found at Christie's flat in June, 1970. The eleven detonators were French, and in every single bomb in the set where pieces could be recovered, according to Mr Yallop, the detonators were French. The thirty-three sticks of gelignite were also French. Jetex fuel, Bostik glue, resistance plates, fuse wire, batteries, charges, and other bits and pieces found in the flat could be used, in the opinion of experts, for the manufacture of a bomb exactly similar to some of those in the set.

The crucial piece of evidence found in the flat was the John Bull printing set. It was the actual printing set used to stamp each of the Angry Brigade communiqués.

All this, said Mr Mathew, the jury might think was "sufficient evidence to completely and utterly connect certainly the first four defendants with conspiracy to cause, anyway, some of the explosions".

But there was more, particularly from the documents found in the flat, many of which were in the handwriting of the defendants.

There were long lists of the names and addresses of persons prominent in public life, particuarly in politics, industry, the police and the law. Some of them, or the buildings they lived in, were the targets for previous attacks. There were plans of the houses of prominent people—Sir John Eden, a Minister for Technology, Mr Woodrow Wyatt. There was a plan of the house of one of the largest property owners in London, Mr Freshwater. "These plans," said Mr Mathew, "in the sub-mission of the Crown were clearly plans drawn up for the purpose of considering them as targets for future bombings."

There were also essays, articles, mostly typed, with instructions in the use of explosives, firearms, and electronics. There were notes, essays, and various literature advocating violence in politics. There were documents of one type or another which, in the submission of the Crown, clearly showed that these persons were concerned with and interested in not only explosives, but detonators and guns.

Mr Mathew then asked the jury to look at their copy of the Angry Brigade "Moonlighter Cell" communiqué. It was stamped with the same printing set as the others. The draft for the final three lines was found at Amhurst Road: "Now they are killing to defend these profits. The Angry Brigade advises the British ruling classes to get out of Ireland and take their puppets Lynch, Faulkner, etc., with them." It was in Anna Mendelson's handwriting, said Mathew. "Anna Mendelson's handwriting on a draft of a communiqué that bore the Angry Brigade John Bull stamp."

At the same time a typewriter was found in the flat which had been used to type out the Moonlighters' communiqué and the one before it, communiqué eleven, which began, "Davies is a lying bastard . . ."

"A Roneo machine was found which had Roneod them, stencils were found which had been used for copying and so were carbons. And so, members of the jury," Mathew went on, "there can be no doubt, in the submission of the Crown, that these last two communiqués emanated from that flat, and therefore the Crown say, undoubtedly, so did the nine earlier ones which were printed on the same machine."

But there were still two of the defendants Mathew had not managed to tie in with Amhurst Road and the whole conspiracy—the first was Angela Weir. Special Branch men whose job it had been to sort out the material at the flat had found the cover for a British Rail Day-Excursion ticket. It had been issued on 19 August, 1971, by Sealink Travel Limited at Victoria Station. After extensive inquiries, the Special Branch managed to trace the ticket itself, and discovered that it was one of a pair issued together. The return halves of both tickets were also recovered, so there was ample evidence to show that two people on 19 August had travelled to Boulogne for the day. As the cover for one of those tickets was found at Amhurst Road

Anna Mendelson, sentenced to ten years' imprisonment for conspiracy to cause explosions

Hilary Creek, sentenced to ten years' imprisonment for conspiracy to cause explosions

John Barker, sentenced to ten years' imprisonment for conspiracy to cause explosions

Jim Greenfield, sentenced to ten yea[r]s imprisonment for conspiracy to cause explosions

Commander Ernest Bond, who led the police team during the Angry Brigade inquiries, with Detective Chief Superintendent Roy Habershon at a press conference at Scotland Yard after the trial. Both have since been promoted.

on 20 August, clearly one person from the flat had been to France the day before.

"Who was it," Mr Mathew asked, "who used that ticket cover found in the flat, and who was it who went with that person on the other ticket? In the submission of the Crown, those two persons will be proved to be the defendant Barker and Miss Weir."

The evidence offered by the prosecution was a photograph on an identity card for a British Rail twenty-four-hour no-passport excursion. That photograph was, they claimed, Weir's. The Crown also suggested that Hilary Creek, who drew three pounds in foreign currency at Victoria Station on 16 August, had gone out to Paris on that day and joined up with Weir and Barker at Boulogne on the 19th. To back up that allegation, the prosecution would produce three items found at the flat in Miss Creek's handbag: a Metro ticket which had been used on 19 August, a French timetable for the Paris–Boulogne train route, and a copy of *Le Monde*—also dated 19 August. The Crown suggested that what happened was this: Barker and Weir went over to Boulogne on 19 August on a day excursion. On the 16th—the day she drew the money at Victoria Station, Miss Creek went to Paris. At some point, the inference went, she made contact with someone who provided the thirty-three sticks of gelignite and then she travelled to Boulogne on the 19th and joined up with Barker and Weir, returning with them that evening. If the jury were to accept the inferences of the French trip—that the Amhurst Road group went over to replenish supplies from their contacts in the First of May Group, then obviously it was another link in the chain that held the associated set together.

But Mathew still had left his third block of evidence—what the defendants themselves said to the police while in custody—"the area of self-incrimination, it might be called". He had already indicated that there was not much evidence in this direction, but Mathew felt that he should go through it in some detail so that the jury might get an idea of the attitude the defendants were taking, "and what they were in fact saying, if anything, about the matters which were put to them".

He began to describe the conversations each of the defendants had with the police officers who arrested them, how each of the defendants had reacted to the questions put to them by

Commander Bond, and their reactions when confronted with the material brought back to Albany Street police station from Amhurst Road. He went over Greenfield's alleged confession about going to France to collect the gelignite, and pointed out that Greenfield had volunteered this information before any of the police officers knew anything about the French trip, before in fact the various pieces of paper, ticket stubs, photographs and the rest had been found and checked out.

At one point, as he was reading out part of the questions and answers in Greenfield's interrogation, there were protests from the dock. Mr Justice James reminded the defendants:

"I think everybody accepts that people in the dock may not agree with the evidence that is being put before the jury by way of opening. But you will all have an opportunity of giving your version, if you want to give it, at an appropriate time. It is hard enough for the jury to sit here and take it in, so please, if you would, try and control yourselves and do not interrupt."

A defendant: "It is a little difficult . . ."

Mr Justice James: "We won't have any argument: just try and control yourselves if you would."

This firm but conciliatory attitude by the judge was to characterise the whole of his conduct at the trial. Throughout all the exasperations to come, Mr Justice James was consistent in his politeness and fairness. Only once did the highly partisan public gallery, so partisan that a Special Branch man was designated to keep watch on them, have occasion to barrack the judge—and that was much later when he questioned the value of Angela Weir's seven alibi witnesses from the Gay Liberation Front. On the whole, though, his way of handling the proceedings did a lot to lower the emotional atmosphere. And that atmosphere was at its worst during the evidence of the "verbals" as they are called.

Verballing, the technique of altering or making up a suspect's statement in order to add weight to the evidence against him, is one of the most contentious areas in relations between the police and the public. What a policeman puts down in his notebook as a record of a conversation he had with a defendant is open to challenge on several counts. For a start, even with the best of intentions, it is rarely absolutely accurate. A detective would have to have the power of total recall if it were to be so. It is also that part of the evidence that *directly* involves the police and the accused. People know what they have told the police, and when they hear a different version given in court, no matter how slight, they are obviously going to react. More so at this trial, partly because it was almost entirely through the verbals that Christopher Bott came to be on trial at all.

Like Angela Weir, he was charged with conspiracy only. The case against him was what he had told police officers after he had been to call at Amhurst Road, his alleged knowledge of dynamite in the flat. There was also some documentary evidence that he had been using the flat. But that, and his association with other defendants, was about all there was against him.

Mathew's opening statement lasted two days. Ahead of the jury lay six months of some of the most complex evidence ever presented to a court. He finished with the hope that what he had said would make it easier for the jury to follow the evidence.

Members of the jury, in order that in due course you can come to your proper consideration, and to your proper verdicts, whatever they may be, in relation to each of these defendants, on each count in this indictment, my learned friend Mr Richardson, my learned friend Mr Smith and I will now call that evidence before you.

CHAPTER ELEVEN

Forensic evidence . . . Cross-examinations . . .
Conspiracy arguments

SOME IDEA OF the massive task the jury had to face was apparent from one look at the statistics involved in the trial papers. The list of exhibits alone ran to twenty-two foolscap pages, containing 688 items. Their range and variety was enormous. From the Beretta sub-machine gun to the imitation US$735, from "plain swab from lower left of door" to "unidentified substance from foot of tree in garden rear of door", from "Butch Cassidy letter to Commissioner" to "copy of applications to re-license motor vehicle 30RKK and notification of change of ownership". There were letters written by the defendants, the communiqués sent after the bombings, sheets of paper with addresses and notes, and of course all the political literature found at Amhurst Road that the prosecution felt was material to the case.

More than two hundred people were down on the list as prosecution witnesses. A good many of them, of course, were simply furnished statements as to the circumstances of given situations, the people who found the various devices, photographers, handwriting experts, fingerprint specialists, journalists from papers which had received communiqués. But for Mathew to "prove" the set, each one had to play his or her part, either by giving evidence in person or by having their statements read out in court.

Much of the early evidence was almost a formality. Descriptions of scenes, detail of procedures, eye-witness accounts. It was not until the big guns from the Woolwich explosives laboratory began to give their evidence that the first real sign of the battles ahead began to emerge.

Mr Howard Yallop took the stand first. His laboratory, and his colleagues at Woolwich Arsenal, have long been regarded as world authorities on explosives and explosive analysis. Mr Yallop himself is the author of several papers on the subject. He described how he had devised his method of detecting what kind of explosive had been used in a particular bomb. The technique was to find the key substances, the basic radicals, at the seat of the explosion—sulphate, ammonium nitrate, chloride, sodium. This was done by analysing traces of material left on the debris. Depending on the result of the analysis, Yallop could then say whether there was TNT, or ammonium nitrate, or nitroglycerine in an explosion, and even the exact proportion of these substances used in the make-up of a bomb.

Armed with this technique, Yallop and his assistant, Mr Lidstone, began to list all the bombs they could find which contained similar explosives. They were even able to say that the proportions of different explosives found in some blasts corresponded exactly to the proportions found in explosives that were standard commercial products in France, and they could name them—Nitramite 19c and Nitratex 4 OR. This, of course, was the make of gelignite recovered intact from some of the bombs that didn't explode.

Having established a chemical link between a certain number of bombs, Yallop and Lidstone began to look for other connections or common factors among the one thousand one hundred police cases which had been through the Woolwich laboratories over the previous four years. Of these, one hundred and nine were in the technical jargon of the scientists and of the court, "infernal machines" used against *property*. Fifteen out of the one hundred and nine were ignited by the acid-delay technique described by Mathew and used in the Carr bombs. But did those fifteen have any other common factors, the scientists asked. Well, they all had proven continental explosives, and in all one hundred and nine infernal machines used against property, only seventeen had detonators. Thirteen of them (all French) were among fifteen bombs with acid delay systems. There were other links through the type of bottle used to hold the acid, many of which were MacCartney serum bottles.

Now, the argument went on, a lot of these characteristics were present in the remaining eight bombs in the set. For a start, there were the same kind of detonators, and the same French explosive, then there was the use of sugar and sodium chlorate to set off the detonators, and of course the nature of the targets was similar. The eight remaining bombs had common factors of their own—the timing devices, the use of alarm clocks, Ever Ready batteries, safety switches, even the methods of connecting the wires.

From all this, Yallop and Lidstone produced an elaborate chart to show that the evidence of all twenty-five bombs in the set being associated was, as Yallop put it, "far beyond reasonable doubt".

This technique of finding associations and proving them by their probability, or at least by the improbability of there being any other explanation, is by no means uncommon. It is used regularly by psychologists and sociologists to show that, say, certain features of upbringing can lead to certain attitudes in later life. Sometimes it is used in medical research to show that drugs produce certain effects, or by archaeologists to show that the same race of prehistoric man occupied two different hill forts. But all that did not impress the defence. They produced an expert witness of their own.

Dr Roy Cahill, MA(Cantab.), Dip.Soc.Admin., cast doubt on the value of the chart and on the validity of the set itself. He said his major preoccupation had been applying his mind and professional expertise to the question of associated sets. He began by making a distinction between established evidence, and evidence based on inference. He said he found both kinds in Yallop's and Lidstone's evidence, and he gave as an example three cases where Lidstone's depositions said no traces of detonators were left, and yet on Yallop's chart there were marks meaning detonators were used. "Where physical pieces of detonators are found, that is well established data, where no pieces are found and inference is drawn that a detonator was used, that is evidence based on inference." Yallop's chart, said Dr Cahill, did not draw a distinction between those two kinds of evidence. The correct statistical practice would be to draw a distinction, "because with data based on inference one cannot be entirely certain that the inference is correct, and that would affect the calculation that would follow". It could lead to considerable uncertainty in the results.

Dr Cahill added that Yallop's choice of features for comparing the bombing incidents seemed to be entirely arbitrary. "We are given no reason," said Dr Cahill, "for the choice of those features rather than any others." There may well have been one, he said, but it wasn't given on the chart. Dr Cahill said Yallop had not used the right statistical tests to establish that the twenty-five bombing incidents were associated with each other. He had used a test which was designed to establish differences. It proved a negative. What Yallop had done, argued Cahill, was to prove that the twenty-five bombings were different from the others he had examined in respect to several arbitrarily chosen features. "If I had chosen other features I would certainly have arrived at a different group."

Essentially, he said, Yallop had proved that the twenty-five were different from the rest but not necessarily similar to each other.

Ian McDonald, Counsel for Greenfield, was even more sceptical in his cross-examination of Yallop and Lidstone. McDonald had with him in the court to advise him on the science of it all, a seventy-five-year-old chemistry lecturer and expert on explosives, Colonel Shaw. They began their attack by contending that the way the prosecution had reached their chemical conclusions, the basic link between the twenty-five bombs, was both "inconclusive" and "unsound". Colonel Shaw went even further when he gave evidence in the witness box. He maintained that the system of analysis used at Woolwich was wholly inadequate and even misleading. In fact, the argument over the correct way to analyse chemical traces after explosions took up several days. McDonald suggested in his cross-examination of Yallop that to try to arrive at a combination of chemicals simply on the basis of what was found at the seat of an explosion could not be done without some kind of "interpretation". Colonel Shaw pointed out that a main weakness of the evidence was the fact that no attempt was made to find out whether any of the chemicals were present away from the site of the explosion. In other words, no control swabs were taken to determine the different levels of contamination. Colonel Shaw also criticised the Woolwich people for failing to carry out a second set of tests to confirm the accuracy of their first analysis.

McDONALD: "Would you expect to find tests done in duplicate in the laboratory with the highest reputation in the world?"
SHAW: "I would expect it in any laboratory."
McD.: "Would you expect the second man in charge of a laboratory with a high reputation to say such things as the

chemical evidence showed ammonium nitrate and sodium chlorate?"

SHAW: "Certainly not."

JUDGE: "I don't see why."

SHAW: "Because he can't say whether that is ammonium nitrate or sodium chlorate."

This attempt by McDonald and Colonel Shaw to throw doubt on to the expert evidence given by the scientists at Woolwich drew an indignant response from Mr Lidstone himself when he was under cross-examination in the witness box:

> I am going to make one statement that I would like to put on record. I come from an explosives forensic establishment which has over one hundred years of active investigation. It is well known all over the world, and we take pride in our accuracy and our integrity, and to suggest that I have the slightest interest in refusing to give any information whatsoever I regard as insulting.

The clash of personality, the polarisation of positions between the defence and the scientists, was nothing compared with what was to come when the senior police witnesses began to give their evidence. It began quietly enough, with the officer in charge of the case, Commander Ernest Bond, answering Mathew's questions on his part in the inquiries. But when McDonald began his cross-examination it soon became clear what line of defence he, and the three representing themselves, at any rate, were taking. It was obvious that they were attempting to turn the whole conspiracy theory on its head, by maintaining that it was the police who had conspired with the Attorney General and members of the Cabinet to make an example of the people on trial. In other words, they were proceeding from the proposition that the whole thing was a political frame up. Bond, Barker suggested, was acting "on orders from above" to smash the Angry Brigade by any means possible, and that was the reason the Bomb Squad had been formed, that was the reason the guns and explosives had been "planted" at Amhurst Road, put there deliberately by the police, because everyone in the team knew results were essential. And why was there this tremendous pressure to "get" the Angry

Brigade? Because, Barker argued, of the threat it posed to authority. Bond, of course, did not agree:

BOND: "The Angry Brigade were dangerous because of the series of bombings they had embarked upon. And I am quite sure that sooner or later we would have had somebody killed. In fact one lady was seriously injured as a result of one bomb. And I think this was the most important danger involved.

BARKER: "Don't you think you are being totally and completely hypocritical when you say that?"

"I am giving you my opinion."

"I suggest that what was thought to be dangerous about the Angry Brigade was not the small amount of explosives they used, but the kind of people their bombs were aimed at?"

"No. The principal danger was the seriousness of these incidents and the ever-present danger that somebody might be killed or seriously injured at least."

Bond's cross-examination, and later Habershon's, turned into a battle of wits over the political issue, with the police officers maintaining that there was nothing exceptional in their investigations, that it was all normal police procedure, and on the other hand the defence trying to insist that the scope of their inquiries was exceptional. They stressed the role of the Special Branch in the inquiries. They asked how many were involved, the number of raids carried out, how many suspects there were, and what kind of people they were. And what kind of people were the Angry Brigade, McDonald asked, what kind of organisation was it?

BOND: "I don't know. I regard the Angry Brigade as an idea that anyone can join."

McDONALD: "An idea, not an organisation?"

"No, sir. I don't accept it as an organisation."

"You said you didn't know what sort of organisation the Angry Brigade was?"

"Right."

"So you don't know how it—if it is an organisation—is actually organised?"

"No."

"Don't know if it has got membership, constitution, chairman, secretary, treasurer?"

"I don't. And I doubt if any of those gentlemen you speak of exist."

"You don't know what its aims and objectives were?"

"I have a good idea."

"You don't know whether there were various branches of the organization or how it was structured?"

"No."

"You don't know whether there were cells or branches in Birmingham, Manchester, Liverpool, London . . .?"

"No. But I can say they have connections in Manchester, Birmingham, Glasgow."

"How can you say they have connections there if you don't know anything about how they were organised?"

"Speaking from knowledge of those who we have encountered and those we have arrested."

"So what you are saying is that the people who have been arrested and encountered know people in those cities? But of course you don't know if it has a membership?"

"Yes (to first question). No (to second)."

"So you don't know if any of the people you have arrested are members?"

"Their membership is established by our inquiries."

"So we are now in the position that you do now actually know that it has a membership?"

"Of course it has a membership."

"Why?"

"Because if there were no members it wouldn't exist."

"But you said earlier in answer that you thought it was more of an idea than an organisation?"

"Yes."

"So if that is true you are not in a position to say whether it has a membership?"

"It has a membership of those we arrested in our inquiries including those for bombings, cheques and such. I am satisfied those we have come across through our inquiries are members of the Angry Brigade."

"But you don't know?"

JUDGE: "Am I understanding you right to say that you, from

your investigations and information, have come to regard the expression 'Angry Brigade' as a name given to an idea or philosophy that anybody can subscribe to if they want to and that those people who say they subscribe to that idea you call members?"

"Yes. It is not like a gang of ordinary criminals that we know all the members and could set out to arrest them. This is an idea, and we only establish membership by our inquiries and arrests in this case."

There is no question that Bond and the rest of the police in the investigation would have been far happier if the Angry Brigade had been like an "ordinary gang of criminals". But as Anna Mendelson pointed out in her cross-examination, they had been referred to by Mathew himself as "anarchists or self-styled revolutionaries". What, she asked, did "self-styled" mean?

BOND: "Adopting a style of your own."
MENDELSON: "Does that mean that all revolutionaries set up a style of their own? Like setting up a business?"
  "It could if that business was bombing."
  "So you think that at some point we decided we would be anarchists?"
  "You decided to adopt that line."
  "What line?"
  "The line of anarchy by enforcing your opinions on others by acts of violence."
  "That is what you think of as an anarchist. Anarchists and self-styled revolutionaries are the same thing."
  "They are anarchists."
  "You would never use the phrase 'self-styled revolutionary'?"
  "I have never used that phrase."
  "What evidence do you have of us setting ourselves up as anarchists?"
  "The evidence before this court quite clearly shows that you were grouped together for this campaign against authority and after all if that is not anarchy I don't know what is."
  "When you say that we were grouped together, do you mean that everybody in this dock is grouped together?"

"Yes."

"Do you mean we are working together as a group?"

"I am saying you are working together in this conspiracy."

But as far as Commander Bond was concerned, by far the most searching part of his cross-examination came when he was taken over, almost line by line, his interrogation of the defendants at Albany Street police station. It was most dramatic in the case of those who were defending themselves. Here they were confronting the people they had been up against, not through the third party of a lawyer, but directly in the courtroom. During the original interrogation, the three police present were Bond himself, asking the questions, Sergeant Davies who was making notes, and John Barker, who challenged the whole procedure:

BARKER: "Mr Davies has down 'I am not signing anything' but I simply said 'No'."

BOND: "The written record is 'I am not making any written statement or signing anything'."

"That is almost word for word what you said Anna Mendelson said. It seems a standard reply for the police making everything sound melodramatic."

"I don't see why 'no' shouldn't have been recorded."

"Perhaps Sergeant Davies wanted to create some kind of impression or he got bored of just putting the word 'no'."

"I can't see any reason for that."

"Page 440 'You remember seeing the holdall'. The answer written down is 'Yes', but I said that I had never seen it before."

"Your recorded answer is 'Yes'."

"But you yourself say that you wouldn't be able to remember them. Despite the fact that I denied knowing about the bag and what was in it. Do you remember saying that I knew about the guns? You didn't want to know about what I knew. Commander Bond, we can go through exactly the amount of times I said it. Did you want to know that I didn't know anything about the guns?"

"You never said that. Had you made the allegations that the property had been planted on you, it would have been recorded."

"You had got the results that you wanted and you didn't want to know about anything else. You were totally indifferent to what I was saying. You went on to say 'Was it there when you looked around the flat six weeks ago?'"

"It would have been recorded."

"You did say it and it wasn't recorded. You went on to ask 'Was it there when you took over the flat six weeks ago?' I replied that 'It seems a peculiar thing doesn't it?'"

"Yes."

"You realise that it was a sarcastic reply."

"It could be such."

"I said that your officers put it there."

"You never said that at all, Mr Barker."

"You also have a considerable degree of power and control in that it is you and your officers who are taking the notes, and there is no independent witness present of what the written evidence is as to what was said in the police station."

"The notes of the interview were taken by Davies in my presence and in the presence of C.I. Wilson."

"You never gave me those notes to read nor asked me whether I agreed that they were a true record?"

"No, I didn't."

"So taken into consideration along with my asking for a solicitor and you saying you wouldn't have allowed one in anyway, that means you have total control over what is written down?"

"No. I don't have total control. I ask the questions. Davies recorded the questions and your answers."

"Davies has the power to put in or leave out things if he wants to? He is the person with the pen and there is nobody there to contradict him?"

"Davies is an experienced officer. I am convinced he made an accurate note."

At least in the case of Commander Bond this complete disagreement with the defendants was carried out in the court with a degree of politeness. It was in contrast with the bitterness that characterised the series of exchanges between those defending themselves and the next major police witness, Detective Chief Superintendent Roy Habershon.

It was Habershon, of course, who had first taken an interest in Ian Purdie and Stuart Christie as suspects because of their previous record of political violence, and it was on this subject that an exchange took place which illustrated the courtroom clash at its strongest.

BARKER: "You said that two of the first people you were interested in before any mention of Jake Prescott were Purdie and Christie?"

HABERSHON: "Yes."

"I suggest to you that finding my name in Manchester which had some connection with Purdie and then finding my name in Christie's address book made me an ideal suspect."

"It made you a suspect . . . I don't know how you describe an ideal suspect."

"By ideal, I mean it was the first name to have connections with both Purdie and Christie?"

"Oh no. I could name you a dozen people in your fraternity which have those same associations."

"Which fraternity is that?"

"The one from which all eight sprang."

"What is that?"

"Well, the revolutionary group which I say you belong to."

"What is that?"

"Well, it is centred largely upon 26 Grosvenor Avenue, 14 Cannock Street, Bridge House, South Horseferry, 4 St Georges Terrace . . ."

"Is it Maoist, anarchist, fascist?"

"I don't wish to put any label on you. A label has been described which you adopted yourselves. You call yourselves the Angry Brigade. That will do for me."

"That is the title *you* have decided on . . ."

JUDGE: "You mustn't shout at him like that. You are just repeating a series of assertions."

"I put it to you that it is in fact you who have decided that all these people who you have grouped together in your mind you call the Angry Brigade or you call them a fraternity."

"You appear to have forgotten for a start the fact that you were found in possession of the stamp which links all the communiqués which were ever issued by that group."

"When you talk about a fraternity you imply that there are a lot more people connected with us. . . . You haven't produced evidence?"

"Indeed there are. If I had the necessary evidence I would charge them."

"And as you haven't the evidence, then you shouldn't make remarks like that."

"I am entitled to have my opinion based on my inquiries."

"But your opinions are rather different to other people's opinions because your opinions have the power of leading people to be falsely imprisoned, don't they?"

"Anyone whom I charge with any offence I have to take before the court the evidence to justify that charge which is then subjected to the closest scrutiny, as you have seen in this court."

"And Purdie, totally on the basis of your opinions, was falsely imprisoned for eight to nine months? Right?"

"No."

"And you made a big blunder with Purdie, didn't you?"

"No."

"You arrest a man, you charge him, you keep him in prison for eight months, and then he is acquitted. That is a blunder?"

"It was a bit of a job to arrest Purdie. As soon as Prescott was arrested he went into hiding. He shaved off his beard and his moustache, changed his name, ran away when we came to the front door. . . ."

"He was acquitted, wasn't he?"

"He was, yes."

"But you think you are God almighty, and if you think he was guilty then he is guilty and any jury who says he is not guilty, that is a mistake, because you know. That is right, isn't it?"

"No, it is not."

That personal attack on Habershon was followed by equally virulent assertions when the police involved in the raid on Amhurst Road came into the witness box. In order to substantiate the allegation of the "plant" the defence had to question the circumstances of the raid in detail. The slightest discrepancy in police evidence was probed, challenged. And in cases where this could not be done, the officers were simply accused of lying.

The questions from the three defending themselves came again, from first-hand knowledge of the situation.

"I was there too, Sergeant Gilham, when you raided the flat," said John Barker on one occasion, reminding the court of his rather unique position. No matter how skilful a professional barrister might be, the effect of this personal confrontation was obviously more forceful, more telling. It was also a way of getting on to personal terms with the jury, and in a case where so much of the evidence was directly disputed, where so many of the situations were "his word against mine", this was clearly important.

Sergeant Gilham, who led the raid, was on the witness stand for a week. His account of what happened was straightforward enough. He and other officers received information from people keeping watch on the flat. They raided it on a search warrant to arrest Greenfield and Mendelson on a cheque charge. They entered the flat and found that John Barker and Hilary Creek were also living there. They admitted that they had heard the names in connection with bombs, but said the raid was not for that reason. Four police officers were in the main bedroom of the flat for three or four minutes while Mendelson and Greenfield were arrested and taken downstairs to a police car in the street. During that time nothing incriminating was seen. Immediately after Mendelson and Greenfield had left, Gilham and Davies began to search the place for stolen cheque books. In the space of a couple of minutes they had found the explosives, the guns and the ammunition. Barker and Creek were then arrested and taken downstairs to wait for a police car to take them to Albany police station. This version of the raid, given by Sergeant Gilham, was supported by Sergeant Davies, but there were slight differences in the evidence of some of the other police officers who took part, and these were seized on by the defence, particularly by John Barker, to back up their contention that he and Hilary Creek were taken downstairs *twice*. He claimed that as soon as Mendelson and Greenfield were taken out of the flat, they followed. After a five or six minute wait they were then taken back upstairs, and only then were they confronted with the material. The inference was, of course, that in this time the

police had spread the stuff around the flat, having brought it up
previously in two holdalls. Sergeant Davies's retort to this
suggestion was "utter rubbish". His cross-examination by
Barker went on:

BARKER: "It's not utter rubbish, Mr Davies, it's the truth, isn't
   it?"
DAVIES: "It is not, it's utter rubbish."
   "So you're saying that we were never taken down twice,
but Mendelson and Greenfield were taken down and we
were kept there."
   "Yes, that is true."
   "That is a lie, Mr Davies."
   "It is not, Mr Barker."
   "In fact, Mr Davies, your whole description of the raid
is a total fabrication. I am now going to go through with
you in the same way Mr Bond was kind enough to go through
with me everything that happened and you can comment.
I'll put it in the form of questions so that you'll be able
to comment. I'm now going to tell you exactly what did
happen in that room which you know as well as I do, Mr
Davies."
   "We both know the truth, Mr Barker, and I am telling the
truth."
   "No, I'm telling the truth, Mr Davies. All right, just let
me go through what really happened, and then perhaps it
may jog your memory. When you first came in, I in fact
didn't see you until about I imagine you'd been in the room
about two or three minutes because I was getting dressed in
the presence of another police officer, who seems to have
mysteriously disappeared from the scene, and he told me to
get dressed. When I went into the large room, Mr Davies, I
saw you sitting at the table having put a piece of paper in
the typewriter, and you were typing on that piece of paper."
   "I did not."
   "Yes you did, didn't you, Mr Davies."
   "I did not."
   "And while you were playing around on the typewriter
Mr Sivell is starting to talk to, no sorry, Mr Gilham is
starting to talk to Anna Mendelson which takes another
couple of minutes, and the rest of you are starting to look

around. You were looking at the typewriter, and Doyle is looking in the far corner, and the detective with ginger hair is looking around the fireplace, yes?"

"No."

"Well, you did go to the bookcase, didn't you?"

"Yes."

"That was after you'd done the typing."

"No, I didn't do any typing."

"You went to the bookcase before Anna and Jim were taken down."

"I can't really remember."

"Well, let's look at what you said before, Mr Davies."

"I can't remember at what stage I went to the bookcase, but I know that I did go to the bookcase."

"You did say, Mr Davies, I'm not saying I noted down all your answers but I remember quite clearly that you said you'd gone and looked at the bookcase before Anna and Jim were taken down, and if you'd gone to look at the book shelves and your story and the rest of your fabricated story is true, you would have inevitably seen those detonators."

"No."

"After about six or seven minutes after you'd first entered, it is only then that Jim and Anna are taken down."

"I'm not sure of the exact lapse of time, but probably about six or seven minutes."

"And then Mr Woolard and some other officers then take us downstairs, that's Hilary and myself, without charging us or anything, we are then taken down the stairs."

"No, you were not."

"So, you would say that it's impossible, would you, that Jim, Anna, Hilary, and myself were, about eight minutes after the raid started, all together all four of us in the hallway downstairs, you say that's impossible?"

"I would say that was impossible, but of course I wasn't there, I was up in the flat."

"Yes, but if what you say is true, Mr Davies, it would be impossible, wouldn't it?"

"I don't know, after you'd left the flat, I don't know what happened to you."

"So for all you know, Anna and Jim might have been kept down in the hallway for about twenty minutes?"

"They were taken out of the flat and taken to Albany Street police station."

"I put it to you, Mr Davies, that in fact what really happened was that Hilary and I were then brought back about five or six minutes later after we had been taken down, and that then you proceed to find things with the speed of a silent film, all in the space of about three minutes."

"Utterly untrue."

"Well, you just said that you found most of the things in about two or three minutes."

"I'm answering your question because you said that 'Hilary and I were brought back after about five or six minutes and then you began to find things', that is not so, we found the property in your presence in that room before you were taken away."

"That is not true, Mr Davies. You see, Mr Davies, that all depends, that bit of your story all depends, on us being taken down once, and Sergeant Woollard has told this court on oath that we were taken down twice. What have you got to say about that?"

"I didn't see you if you did come back up, I can't disbelieve Woollard. I don't know if you were or not, I didn't see you, I didn't hear you."

"Incredible, but you've just said it was a pack of lies what I put to you. But you said you didn't see us come back."

JUDGE: "He said, Mr Barker, in fact, that it was a pack of lies the items were found quickly after the two in the flat had been taken down. I think perhaps I ought to remind you that when Mr Woollard was giving evidence on that part of the story there were some parts of his evidence you yourself accused him of lying."

"That's quite true, quite true, what I'm suggesting is that there's a pretty big inconsistency between two different sets of lies, and I've been asking you to explain that, Mr Davies, and of course as you usually do when you're in a corner, you say you can't remember, you didn't see it, that's true, isn't it?"

"No."

"You're making no effort to remember what happened and you're just repeating out the same story that's been drilled into you, that's been drilled into the other lot, and this is something that you've all agreed on."

"No."

"Your statements are all identical, they all read exactly the same, word for word, in fact when you give your statements you're like three parrots, you go through the same notebook and out come the same words, everything happens in the same sequence, all of it is totally unreal in a ludicrous way, it's true, isn't it?"

JUDGE: "Mr Barker, that's not a question, you know, it's a comment. You're perfectly entitled to make that comment to the jury in your summing-up."

Before the arresting officers had left the stand, there was one other allegation of planting they had to face. It came from Stuart Christie's defence lawyer, Mr Kevin Winstain. He began his cross-examination of Sergeant Gilham by trying to establish a possible motive for a plant.

Wasn't Christie well known as a prime suspect? And particularly after the material had been discovered at Amhurst Road wouldn't he have been high on the list of those the police would wish to interview. The Sergeant agreed. So having suggested why the police might have wanted to implicate Christie, Mr Winstain went on to explain how it might have been done. Say originally there had been thirteen detonators at Amhurst Road. Only eleven were recovered from the flat and one of those was on the floor. How did it get there?

"I've no idea," said Gilham.

WINSTAIN: "Human beings are often subject to temptation, are they not? And isn't it right that you pocketed two detonators? For a later time, against another suspect who might not have incriminating material in his possession or in his home?"

"Not at all."

"And with that little touch of nervousness that such an enterprise might induce in a person, you dropped the 11th, having picked up three."

"I did not, sir."

"And that's how it dropped on the floor?"

"No, sir."

Winstain went on to explain that the first person to turn up at Amhurst Road after the raid was Christie in the Ford

Corsair he shared with Albert Meltzer. After his arrest, the car was taken to Stoke Newington police station, and then Winstain went on:

"At some stage you put those detonators in the boot of his car, didn't you?"

"No."

"Or got some other officer to do it, and I nominate Mr Ashendon or Mr Sivell."

"No, sir."

"Didn't want to risk putting them in the front, you put them in the boot—isn't that right?"

"No, sir."

"Where you knew they would be found in the search?"

This cross-examination of the officers involved in the arrests was crucial to the defence if they were to convince the jury that the police were corrupt enough to engage in what was, in their allegations, conspiracy on a massive scale. It took about a month for all of them to give their evidence and answer the cross-examinations by each of the counsels and by those defending themselves. On a personal level, it was by far the most bitterly contested part of the trial. It served once again to illustrate the lack of any kind of common ground between the authorities and those on trial. The fact that Barker and the others were so articulate in their own defence threw the conflict into greater relief, particularly in relation to the verbals.

BARKER: "It is the police who call Jim Greenfield Jimmy. None of the defendants do."

SIVELL: "I would think most of them (the police) call him Greenfield. It is hardly an endearment. We are not on an endearment basis. We are on a very practical basis."

"The point is that you used Christian names and diminutives as a form of humiliation. It is totally grotesque being called by your Christian name by somebody like you."

"My friends don't think so."

"I am not convinced that you have any friends."

"I don't think that is any concern of yours."

Throughout all this Mr Justice James was mild and tolerant. He allowed most of the lines of cross-examination and unlike

Mr Justice Melford Stevenson in the Prescott/Purdie trial, he did not insist that the defence "keep politics out of it". He gave the three defending themselves a lot of leeway, advising them, pointing out their rights, but he also reminded them when they complained about a particular point that they were representing themselves from their own choice. He told John Barker off for swearing, and on another occasion had to remind him that the purpose of cross-examination was to challenge evidence, not to have a roving investigation into a witness's personal views.

So far, the conflicts in the trial had been almost entirely about the evidence, about the veracity of witnesses who were lying, and if so, why; about the soundness of the science and the statistics. The next clash came at the end of the prosecution case with legal arguments over the nature of the conspiracy charge itself. Fortunately for the jury, already battered with three months of facts, it took place without them.

First, the Judge heard a submission on the conspiracy count from Mr Glasgow, for Kate McLean. He said he wished to question whether there was an overall conspiracy at all. The way the Crown put it, "the sort of conspiracy we have here is of a continuing series of events, which, if proved, is a conspiracy people can come in and out of".

The prosecution had given evidence of an associated set of incidents, which was not the same as saying they were a conspiracy. And even if there were one central theme running right through, there must also be joint conspirators who link the conspiracy as a whole. At best, in this case, there was one central theme with no conspirators to link it up.

Mr Mike Mansfield, for Angela Weir, took up the argument that the Crown had failed to prove that the associated set was a conspiracy. He reminded Mr Justice James of Mr Yallop's cross-examination.

> I asked him if in fact there was, from a forensic point of view, one theme or idea behind these incidents. His answer was that there wasn't. The basis of his evidence was the linking of groups *within* the twenty-five bombings.

The Judge asked Mr Mathew to deal with these points first.

As for the submission, said Mathew, that the evidence could disclose more than one conspiracy, it was "misconstrued".

The Crown alleged that there was one conspiracy to cause explosions and it had not been kept to a particular type of target. The jury could, if they wished, come to the view that, say, the first six bombs in the set were not part of the conspiracy. That did not mean that there was not a conspiracy involving each one, or some of the defendants that came into being at a later date. Provided the jury was satisfied that there was a conspiracy that involved two or more of the defendants, then this count was good in law. Mathew went further. If the jury were to find that in fact bombs twelve, thirteen, fourteen and fifteen were in the submission of the Crown nothing whatever to do with the Angry Brigade conspiracy, that did not make the count bad in law, it merely meant that the Crown had proved matters of evidence "which have not in fact been found to be included in the ambit of the conspiracy". To make the count bad, Mathew argued, there would have to be a central figure in the conspiracy and these defendants would have to have been all unknown to each other. "In any event," Mathew finished by saying, "there is abundant evidence on which the jury can be invited to say that there is in fact one conspiracy in existence dating from the first date as alleged in the indictment." But even if the jury were to come to the conclusion that there was a conspiracy to cause explosions, but that it did not start until a later date, say, from bomb number ten, the conspiracy count was nevertheless a good one.

It was Mr Ian McDonald, Jim Greenfield's counsel, who led defence protests at Mathew's interpretation of the conspiracy charge. With some indignation, he said:

What the Crown is alleging in the indictment is that there was a conspiracy to cause explosions between 1 January, 1968, and August, 1971, and the Crown has laid evidence in this case that that is what the conspiracy is. That was their purpose in calling Mr Yallop and having elaborately prepared evidence put before the court and the jury.

What Mr Mathew is now saying is that it doesn't really matter what the Crown alleges in Count one, and it doesn't really matter about its extent. That doesn't really matter: it is up to the jury to find that there was in existence an entirely different conspiracy to the one the Crown alleges—a conspiracy of nine or ten explosions, not twenty-five.

McDonald went on to say that the offence of conspiracy was the cause of some unease in the legal profession because, unlike a specific offence, it was a little bit vague and uncertain. If one took Mr Mathew's arguments to their logical conclusion, then really it would become totally unnecessary in a conspiracy case for the Crown to give particulars of precisely what the limits are of the conspiracy being alleged against the defendants.

Having elected for a conspiracy from 1968 to 1971, then the Crown must prove that conspiracy, McDonald argued. They must then go on and prove that the defendants participated in that conspiracy. Failure to prove the conspiracy in the indictment or suggesting that the evidence amounted to more than one conspiracy made the count bad in law: "The Crown can't have its cake and eat it."

John Barker's line on the conspiracy charge was also legalistic. He said it appeared to be a formalisation of what are called TIC's—things taken into consideration. Someone appears to have looked back from August, 1971, to some cases which have similarities, and they have all been put into one conspiracy. It was no good saying that it did not really matter whether any of the defendants were in at the start of the conspiracy or whether they came into it later. It did matter because the jury had heard a lot about the earlier bombs. It was clearly more serious to be found guilty of a conspiracy covering three and a half years and twenty-five bombs than one which was broken up into bits and pieces. "I don't think the prosecution argument on those lines is valid," Barker concluded.

But it was Mathew who won the day.

The judge rejected the submissions, saving his direction on the rival conspiracy contentions for his summing up, and so on 3 October, 1972, more than three months after the start of the trial, McDonald rose to his feet to make his opening address for the defence of Jim Greenfield.

CHAPTER TWELVE

Defence . . . Closing speeches . . . Summing-up

BY NOW McDONALD, through his aggressive, and impressive, cross-examinations on behalf of Greenfield, had won the confidence of the three defending themselves, and had become their unofficial counsellor as well. What he said in Opening stood for what the others would be arguing themselves. He said the jury must have a pretty good idea by now from the many cross-examinations they had heard, of what the defendants were going to say. But he hoped they would pay the same kind of attention to their evidence as they had to the prosecution's.

The trial, said McDonald, was obviously no ordinary trial. There were not many where political motive was something of importance, and it obviously was in this trial, for two reasons. There were twenty-five bombings alleged as part of the conspiracy count, and the police and prosecution did not have a clue who had actually planted any of the bombs. "Probably no one will have a clue who the real bombers are until they write their memoirs, if they do." Because of this lack of concrete evidence, then, motive became especially important.

Secondly, on the possession charges, motive was crucial because the prosecution had to show that the people in the dock were the sort of people who would logically have guns and explosives in their flat, that they were the kind of people who believed in the use of guns and bombs. If you were going to plant someone with explosives and the rest, it was no good picking on lifelong pacifists.

"Finding people with the right political motives has been one of the main focuses of the police investigation in the Angry Brigade bombing."

Another reason why the trial was out of the ordinary was the kind of victims of the different bombings—two Cabinet Ministers, a Chief of Police, a captain of industry. Whatever Bond had said in the witness box, it must have been obvious, McDonald suggested, to anyone looking at the facts, that there was tremendous pressure on the police to smash the Angry

Brigade. And smashing the Angry Brigade was not just a question of arresting them.

> It goes much further than that. It means ensuring that those whom the police arrested are taken to court and that the key people, which is the Amhurst Road four, are convicted and sent to prison. And this is where you, the jury, come in. If the powers-that-be have their way, then your task is to convict these defendants—maybe letting off one or two of the peripheral ones—and then the press and everyone can bray triumphantly about how successful the police have been in tracking down these red hippie hooligans, or whatever other epithets Fleet Street think up in describing them. Make no mistake, that is what the powers-that-be expected and hope for in this case. Your co-operation is part of that overall strategy. And I believe that is what is expected of you in this case. You probably realise by now that the verdict you have to give in this trial is of concern to more people than simply the relatives of those in the dock. You probably realise that the whole British Establishment awaits your verdict with bated breath. You and the defendants, when you really consider it, are the only unpredictable factors in this whole scenario. The rest of us can be expected to play our allotted parts. That gives you enormous power. It is your decision, and your decision alone, that decides the outcome of this case.

McDonald warned the jury not to be overawed by the proceedings, past and future.

> When you first come to this court, you probably find that you are in totally unfamiliar surroundings. You come and find us all dressed up in wigs and gowns talking in a very strange language and you feel totally bewildered, and your first reaction is probably to sit there and when people tell you to go somewhere, you go somewhere. Someone says, "Get in the lift and go to the jury room and stay there until I get you."
> Then during the course of the trial you have had to sit and not say a word. I can have a row with Mathew or get heated with a witness, and you have to sit and take it. You are not allowed to say anything at all during the course of the trial. Again you may become quite passive and sit there and take

it, and you might forget that you have all the power at the end of the trial to deliver a verdict.

Again there is the court procedure. Everything when you come into the court seems to revolve around the Judge. He is the person who gives directions in relation to procedure. He is the person who when he comes into court we all stand up. When he sits down, we sit down. It may feel that all power in the court is centred on him, sitting up there in an elevated position half-way up the wall. You may feel that you are not the people who have all the power. I only say that because so far as the procedure in the court is concerned, those of us who are here, including the Judge, are here to help and guide you, but in the end none of us have any power over you. Whatever I say, when I close the case for Greenfield, you are entitled to ignore it completely. And if you think I am talking a lot of nonsense, you must ignore it. Similarly, when the Judge is summing up at the end of the case, if you think what he is saying is a lot of nonsense, you must ignore that too.

JUDGE: "They can't. Not on the Law."

"But his view of the facts you can. That is your power. I want to emphasise that, because during the next few weeks you are going to hear a lot of evidence, and I want you to remember that."

After his opening statement, McDonald called Greenfield into the witness box. He took him through his early life, his academic career, his reactions to Cambridge, and his reasons for leaving. In detail, Greenfield went over his movements after he had come to London, where he was and what he was doing when each of the bombs in the set was laid, including those at Paddington and Manchester, which, the prosecution alleged, had his fingerprints on the wrappings.

A large part of Greenfield's evidence was taken up with the political motive behind his actions. He explained the work they had all been doing on the newspaper *Strike*, what his particular contribution on the "repression industry" meant. Greenfield did not deny that he was sympathetic to the Angry Brigade. In the class war they were on the same side as he was, but he disapproved of their bombs because as far as he could judge, they did nothing to advance the cause of the working class. He put forward the explanation that each of the defendants from Amhurst Road gave to explain the existence of the Angry Brigade material found in the flat.

The John Bull printing set, for example, had been brought there by two people who were connected with the Angry Brigade. They had used the duplicator at the flat to print Communiqué 11. They knew the people living there would not give them away to the police.

While they were there, Greenfield had asked them if they knew anything about the Davies bomb, which had gone off some days before. They said they had not done it themselves, but they knew who did. It was because of this interest shown by Greenfield that they sent him the document on guns and explosives found in the flat by the police.

As for the guns and ammunition, well, it had already been explained how they had got there, except that Greenfield developed the police moves further. Someone in the Angry Brigade group had talked too much. The police got to know that there were incriminating documents at Amhurst Road. They already had the arms cache, taken from premises elsewhere. The flat was the obvious place to put it.

As for the rest of the evidence found there, most of it was part of the research the four at Amhurst Road were doing into how the power structure in Britain really worked. They did not think there was enough information available to ordinary people on such things as how companies were structured, the links between them, and the links between the people who managed them. The Freshwater group of companies, for example, stood to make a fortune out of the Housing Finance Act. The people at Amhurst Road felt the company were pressurising the Government to implement the Bill as soon as possible. They set out to make inquiries into who was who on the Board, where they lived, what sort of lifestyle they had. That was why, the defendants argued, there were so many plans and lists in the flat. They certainly were not potential bombing targets.

The lists of names of other prominent people found at Amhurst Road were part of what they called "reverse sociology". Sociologists were always analysing working class areas—Notting Hill for example was inundated with them. It amounted to spying and control by the authorities. Barker, Greenfield and the others wanted to reverse the process by analysing a middle class ghetto. To do this, they had to find out where people like judges and others in authority had their clubs, who they mixed with. "We wanted to pick out people who we considered to be important and see how they fitted together." They could then be fitted into a background, a power centre, like Chelsea. The work was still in a raw state when they were arrested. But they were hoping eventually to use all the material in a series of pamphlets or broadsheets.

Mathew wasted no time when he rose to cross-examine:

"Well, Mr Greenfield, who are these two mysterious people who suddenly turn up at 359 Amhurst Road?"

"I don't intend to tell you."

"Why is that?"

"Because I don't feel they should be put in the same position I am in now."

"But it is they who have largely contributed, if there is a word of truth in what you say, they are the people who have largely contributed to you being where you are today."

"The people who are responsible for putting me where I am today are the policemen who planted all the . . ."

"All the incriminating property found at Amhurst Road. . . . Why do you wish to protect them, Mr Greenfield?"

"I wish to protect them because, criticism aside of the Angry Brigade, what they may have done, what they may have had in mind, criticism of that aside, in opposition to you, they are on my side."

"Terrorists?"

"No, I wouldn't say they are terrorists, but it is open to debate."

Mathew pressed on with this line of questioning:

"You, Mr Greenfield, using violence by bombing, if you thought that would have helped your ideals, would you have resorted to it?"

"I wasn't interested in advancing my ideals."

"I thought you had been telling us very little else for the past two days. You left university and did very little work just to do this."

"What I have done is attempting over the last few years to live and act in a way that I would call socialist. I am not interested in propagating my ideals."

"Would I be right in suggesting that you didn't want to tell us the names of the two people, and what you have said is quite untrue?"

"You are getting paid to say that. What I have said is perfectly true."

"The reason you won't tell us these names is because you know that what you have said in this court is quite untrue."

"I know that I have told the truth."

"One other general matter before we come down to the facts in this case. I don't think we have argued about this. You have a hatred of the police, haven't you?"

"No, what I do have is, I have had certain experiences which allow me to put the police in perspective inside the modern state, and I see how and why they do certain things."

"And are you telling this court that as far as you are concerned you don't hate the police?"

"I hate the people who came to Amhurst Road and planted us with guns and explosives. In general, I don't hate the police at all."

"You had some unfortunate experiences at Widnes when you were arrested . . ."

"Yes."

"And in August?"

"Yes."

"And you saw some unhappy things happening at Notting Hill Gate."

"Unhappy!"

"Did you see unhappy things happen?"

"I would say it was downright disgusting."

"That is what I thought you would say. You hate the police."

"That is not enough."

"And when you started to put together this periodical called *Strike* you were dealing with matters under the heading 'Repression'."

"Yes."

"And what I suggest to you, Mr Greenfield, is this. That really such is your hatred of the police and authority in general, but particularly the police . . ."

"What authority?"

"I am talking about the police in particular."

"You also mention authority, and I would like to know which authority you mean."

"Unfortunately you will interrupt when I haven't finished the question. You see, Mr Greenfield, you really have to dispute and attack the police in everything they say and do as you have in this case."

"I have to do it because everything they say and do that I have disputed is fabricated."

In all his cross-examinations, Mathew took the same line: the defendants had nothing to lose by calling the police liars, after all it was the only defence they had in the face of such a mass of evidence. Not, of course, that anyone in the dock agreed with that. Barker began his defence with a ten-thousand-word monologue which was almost a complete political testament. He did not have counsel to help him through with a series of questions and replies as Greenfield had had. But fluently, without interruption, he sketched out his early life, the things that had conditioned his political thinking. He went over his experiences with the Claimants Union, his involvement with the current political scene, although throughout, Barker, and the rest, avoided defining their political beliefs too specifically. They never used the word "anarchist"—all except Christie, that is, who was already known as one. The nearest definition of themselves they offered was libertarian socialist.

What Barker tried to do with the jury was to convince them that there was nothing sinister in the various documents the prosecution had produced as evidence. He claimed that they were part of a logical and legitimate political process, even if it was one that the jury, certainly, and most other people in court were probably hearing for the first time:

I thought what was wrong with the A.B. was that it didn't seem to be a general campaign or strategy, and I have always believed that the only way you are going to get anywhere worthwhile is when a lot of people have actually reached the stage in their everyday experience of wanting to use class violence. They can't just say we are going to introduce it and see what happens because that is what I call

elitism, they are saying that we have decided to do this and
see what will happen completely out of time with what is
happening generally. Mainly I think despite all my political
criticisms, I did respect the people in the A.B. because they
were at least putting into practice what they thought to be
right or what they believed to be happening at that time,
but I came to the conclusion that really I couldn't become a
part of it (1) because I didn't really have the necessary kind
of experience, and (2) because I thought it would be a full
time thing, and I certainly don't believe something that
what the A.B. is doing is worth doing full time, and thirdly I
ask myself the question, is this the time to do this sort of
thing, and I came to the conclusion that it wasn't and that all
that it was really producing was an excuse for a terrible
amount of repression amongst people who had the same
kind of ideas on the same kind of thing as myself.

Without condemning their ideas out of hand, Barker was, at
the same time, trying to dissociate himself from them. It was
a narrow path, and one that he trod in relation to most of the
documentary evidence at Amhurst Road.

On the list of addresses the prosecution alleged were targets
for robbery, Barker agreed that he had thought about robbery.
He had made a few notes on the possibilities, but it had never
got further than that. Writing it down was more of an excuse
for inactivity. Barker also explained about the trip to France.
It was true that Hilary Creek went to Paris on 16 August. But
she went there to talk to someone about the possibility of
setting up an information service. Barker himself was approached that same day by one of the two Angry Brigade
people who had been using the flat. He was asked whether he
would take a message to a contact in Boulogne. It was about a
plan to house Purdie and Prescott after they had been sprung
from prison, should they be convicted. He had written down
details of the message so he would remember it. That was the
note the police had found. He admitted that Rosemary Pink
was not the real name of the girl who went with him. But it
certainly was not Angela Weir, as the prosecution alleged.

Mathew discovered during his cross-examination that Barker
and all of the defendants had careful explanations for all the
evidence offered against them, no matter how incriminating it

might seem. How plausible they sounded to the jury had to wait on their verdict. But it was plain by now that it was really going to be a case of whose word to believe. There was virtually no common ground.

In the case of the four sitting in the second row in the dock, the ones who did not live at Amhurst Road, no one suggested that the flat material belonged to them, even though they were accused of knowing about it. Stuart Christie's counsel, Kevin Winstain, disposed of the main prosecution witness against him —Lisa Byer. She said she had seen Christie with ammunition, heard him talk about the Carr bombs as if he knew more than he could say. But as most of the evidence was uncorroborated in the end, it came down to his word against hers. Counsel for Chris Bott, Angela Weir, and Kate McLean were concerned primarily with dissociating them from the conspiracy in terms of the way it seemed to be defined in law. How could Kate McLean, for example, be involved in a conspiracy that began when she was still a schoolgirl?

But it was defence pleas from the three defending themselves that provided the emotional closing stages.

All the defendants had spent hours preparing their closing speeches. They had been allowed to meet each other, to get together at Brixton to work something out. After all, if they were charged with a conspiracy that involved them all, then the defence against that conspiracy also involved them all. The trouble was that the meetings in prison usually turned into a social occasion rather than the meeting of legal minds, though some work did get done, obviously.

Barker, Creek and Mendelson were to face the jury in person, and after six months in Number One Court, these were to be the moments that really mattered.

Anna Mendelson was the first to get up. She was obviously tired. She had been ill several times throughout the trial and now, as she began her final address, she had to break off from time to time. She began by telling the jury that to understand her arguments they had to understand the way she lived, and the political work she was doing. Only in that way would they see why it was that she had been "planted" with guns and explosives and charged with conspiracy. The prosecution, she said, had two main pieces of evidence against her—the fingerprints found on a copy of *Rolling Stone*, the paper the police say they found in the carrier bag which contained the unexploded Manchester bomb, and secondly the lines she had written for the Angry Brigade Moonlighters' Cell communiqué.

Miss Mendelson said she did not deny that her fingerprints were on the magazine, but she told the jury to remember that she was living at Wivenhoe in Essex at the time, near the university:

> The doors were open, people were always coming in, and half the time you didn't know who they were. There were a lot of strangers around . . . and fingerprints can get on a piece of paper in a million different ways. I can't account for that, and I can't say how it got there. I suppose it just comes down to whether you believe me. I wasn't making bombs.

She also pointed out that she had produced witnesses who testified that she was two hundred miles away in Wivenhoe when the Manchester bomb was laid. These alibi witnesses had not been seriously challenged by the prosecution.

On the second piece of principal evidence against her, the Moonlighters' Cell communiqué, Miss Mendelson said she agreed it had been printed on the Amhurst Road duplicator. But she stressed that there was no evidence to suggest that the communiqué was connected with a bombing. She reminded the jury that many people in Britain were angry about the British government's introduction of internment without trial in Northern Ireland. It was because of this deep feeling that she and the others had against internment that she had helped in the production of a "statement" about it.

No one at Amhurst Road, she went on, had ever denied having contacts with people who said they were the Angry Brigade. They knew many of the people the police had investigated as a result of the bombings, and this made them ideal victims for the plant. They had been singled out because of their past association with people the police had arrested on bombing charges—Prescott and Purdie.

"We might as well get this cleared up," she said, "I was not engaged in any plots or conspiracies with Ian Purdie or Jake Prescott."

As for the Angry Brigade itself, Miss Mendelson quoted the

words of Commander Bond. It was an idea, a philosophy, rather than an organisation. Certainly, said Miss Mendelson, she would never have written out a membership form, because that would have been a positive step towards something she did not want, "which was bombing". In her final plea, Miss Mendelson continued:

> Our sort of people, our politics, the people living in Amhurst Road, we didn't and we don't feel that there is any need or room for bomb attacks on cabinet ministers, although we might understand the feelings behind them. Bombing a cabinet minister isn't going to get rid of the capitalist system, because there is always somebody to step into his place unless the situation and conditions are right.

Anna Mendelson finished her speech with this appeal:

> If you convict us, we are not going to change. We will still be who we are, and what we believe. I know that the people in this dock with me are working together for a happier and more peaceful world. That is who we are. It is your decision.

It was a weary and rather sad Miss Mendelson who sat down to the congratulations of the seven others with her in the dock. Throughout the day and a half she had been on her feet, the jury had listened intently and with apparent concentration, as they did when the next defendant got up—John Barker.

In one sense, his closing speech was a *tour de force*. He had prepared it meticulously, and though he told the jury at one stage that he did not have to prove his innocence—that was in effect what he ended up trying to do. He carefully explored all the different possibilities of the evidence against him, weighing it up, and pointing out the importance to the prosecution case of the evidence he was rejecting. So scrupulous was his analysis, so thorough, that even seasoned lawyers who heard him were impressed. In fact, one counsel was heard to remark that people were paid £15,000 a year for doing precisely what Barker was doing for the first time.

He dealt with the conspiracy charge first. It depended, he said, in the case of the Amhurst Road four, on the association between them and the people who had produced the Moon-lighters' Cell communiqué. But that association, he said, had not involved an agreement to cause explosions. Association with people who said they were active in the Angry Brigade was not synonymous with conspiracy to bomb. The prosecution had twisted all the research work they had been doing at Amhurst Road into an allegation that it provided documentary proof of their involvement in a conspiracy to bomb, so giving the lie to the defence that the explosives had been planted. But Barker pointed out that you could look at it the other way round. Without the explosives, most of the documents would have been irrelevant—hence the need to plant them.

In answer to Mathew's question as to why they hadn't mentioned the possibility of a plant before the trial, Barker said:

> If you make allegations in a magistrates' court, the response is "that it is for the jury to decide", and that is absolutely right. It is for you to decide and not for anyone else. And that is why I have waited, sometimes patiently, to put my side of things to the people who matter. You are the twelve independent people who live in the real world. And you are the people with the power. You are the first people I have come across in any of the courts who have the power to acquit or convict. So the question of a plant is for you.

Barker went to some lengths to try to convince the jury that the raid on Amhurst Road was far from a normal raid, following up a routine fraud inquiry, as the police had maintained. If it was routine, why was it conducted under the command of Bond, the head of the Bomb Squad? If it was a genuine fraud inquiry, why was it not done by the local CID stationed just a few hundred yards away at Stoke Newington police station? If the raid was for cheques, why was the raiding party composed of men from the Bomb Squad? The whole cheque thing, said Barker, was a smokescreen to cover the real aim of the raid—to arrest two very important suspects whom they had never been able to interrogate before. It was also a smokescreen for "the whole amazing thing of discovering these explosives as unexpectedly as possible. They are trying to say that finding the explosives was a complete surprise, but that could only stand up if the raid was normal. There was overwhelming evidence that it wasn't."

Barker suggested that the reason Bond and Habershon were

not there was because they wished to appear to have nothing
to do with the plant.

And why did the authorities resort to such desperate measures
—because of political pressure to "get" the Angry Brigade.

The appearance of arresting people is as important, if not
more important, than actually smashing the Angry Brigade
itself. It's the whole question of setting an example. Showing
people that they can't get away with it. But of course, if that
is the case, they may still be worried about the real Angry
Brigade, perhaps they are still looking for it. They still have a
large Bomb Squad which doesn't seem to have changed much
in size from when we were arrested.

In answer to the charge that, since they had been arrested, the
bombing had stopped, Barker said the Angry Brigade might
have decided it was not worth continuing if the price of bombing
was the arrest of eight innocent people who were politically
active in other ways. Perhaps the Angry Brigade no longer saw
bombings as relevant. Particularly in 1972 with the miners'
strike and the dockers' action around the Industrial Relations
Bill:

Perhaps they now feel that bombs are completely irrelevant,
and that the class war is being fought, and that the Angry
Brigade doesn't have to make symbolic gestures with bombs
to make it real, because it is real.

After Barker's exhaustive analysis, it was Hilary Creek's turn
to address the jury for the last time. She developed some of the
inconsistencies that Barker had pointed out in the prosecution
case. She talked at length about the mass of documents and
research work going on at the flat which the prosecution were
saying was evidence of a conspiracy. They can only do that,
she said, because of the planted explosives. She spent some time
explaining why the conspiracy charge was so important. She
said it put the defendants in the position of having to prove
their innocence. It was a charge that put on trial intangibles
like thoughts and motives. The jury should look at all the
evidence and place it within the context of the court.

We have all been sitting here for six months, and I think you know us. We have talked about ourselves, our politics, and how we carried them out. We told you that that was not by bombing. You have seen us react to questioning. You have heard me speak. I am not an actress. If I am, then I must be the finest in the world and due for an Oscar to have done what I have done for the past six months.

You see the Bomb Squad is still in existence, the same as it was sixteen months ago. It is also admitted that they are still looking for four people. Although they might have been getting close with us, the fact still remains that they got the wrong people, and that's not good enough.

When Hilary Creek sat down at the end of her closing speech, the first four defendants had had their last say. It had taken eight days in total. And it was apparent now that the Amhurst Road four were the centre of the whole case. Counsel for Christie, Bott, Weir and McLean spent little time elaborating what they had already given in defence of their clients. By now the trial had established a record as the longest hearing this century. And there was still the summing up from Mr Justice James, one of the most difficult perhaps that any judge has had to face.

Mr Justice James began by outlining his role in the proceedings. First, on the interpretation of the law, the jury could not ignore him. If he gave a direction in this area they had to accept it. His second task was "to help them as to the facts". But on this, if the jury did not agree with him, they were perfectly entitled to throw his suggestions out of the window.

The Judge freely admitted that to try to sum up the facts, statements and comments of the entire six months was impossible without keeping the jury for many more weeks. It would be his job to pull the evidence together. So he would select what he regarded as relevant. He would lay down the guidelines as to what could be admitted as evidence. This was particularly difficult for him in this case as most of the witnesses for the defence had given much more evidence about "lifestyle" than they had about fact. Indeed, the relevance of one to the other was itself an issue. And when the jury made up their minds about witnesses, they should do so on the basis of "truth, accuracy, and credibility". "Because," he warned, "some people are lying in this case, and there's no getting away from that."

As to the burden of proof, that still lay with the prosecution. And as an example he said it was not necessary for Angela Weir to prove she had been in London on 19 August—the day the police say she was in France collecting explosives—although she had provided seven witnesses from the Gay Liberation Front, who said she had been on a demonstration with them. The prosecution had to prove that she had travelled to France that day.

Mr Justice James turned to the eleven charges. He suggested the jury dealt with them in a specific order, taking the possession charges involving the Amhurst Road four first. That was count five, possessing explosives. After they had made up their minds about that, they should move on to nine, ten and eleven which alleged possession of machine guns, ammunition, detonators and the rest. Having reached a decision on this, they should turn next to the possession charge against Stuart Christie, the two detonators found in his car. Then they should consider counts two and three involving Greenfield's and Mendelson's fingerprints on the Paddington and Italian bombs. Having reached some decision on all of these, they should turn finally to the most important charge—conspiracy.

The Judge, then, was asking the jury to make up their minds, before anything else, on whether the guns and explosives at Amhurst Road had in fact been planted as the defence had maintained. If they believed that they had, then all the rest of the charges started to tumble, and they could not find any of the defendants guilty on anything. But if this first charge held, the Judge seemed to be saying, then the next one could, and so on. It was a kind of domino theory he was suggesting. Mr James's direction was quite clear. "If you decide that the truth is that these police quite wickedly planted these things at the flat, then you could not find the defendants guilty."

Next the Judge dealt with the most complex and difficult part of the case—the conspiracy charge itself. The offence, he said, lies in the agreement. And even if that agreement was *not* put into effect, it was still an offence. The Crown did not have to prove that any of the eight actually caused any of the explosions, simply that they agreed to.

As long as you know what the agreement is, then you are a

conspirator. You needn't necessarily know your fellow conspirators, nor need you be always active in the conspiracy.
All you need to know is the agreement. It can be effected by
a wink or a nod, without a word being exchanged. It need have
no particular time limit, no particular form, no boundaries.

The Crown was charging the eight with agreement to conspire
from January, 1968, to August, 1971, covering an associated set
of twenty-five bombings. If the Crown had proved that, all well
and good. They would have done what they set out to do. But
if they had not succeeded in proving the agreement to the extent
"forecast", in other words for the whole period—but had
proved that there was one agreement to which each of the
defendants had been party for part of the period, then that
would be enough, they would have proved that an agreement
existed, and the eight could be found guilty.

What complicated the situation further was Mr James's
direction that if there was more than one agreement to conspire
in the three and a half year period (the defence had suggested
there were six separate ones), then the defendants were not
guilty. The Judge told the jury that it did not matter if the
defence and the prosecution differed in their interpretation of
conspiracy. "You don't have to decide between rival contentions. You have to follow my directions."

Next, Mr James tried to sort out whether the trial was, as
the defence maintained, a political trial. He was categoric:
"This is not a political trial. Political trials are trials of people
for their political beliefs which happen to be contrary to those
in government. . . . We do not have them in this country."

He felt it necessary to "correct" the impression given by
Ian McDonald, Jim Greenfield's counsel, that the prosecution
itself had been a political decision taken by the Cabinet through
its legal adviser, the Attorney General, Sir Peter Rawlinson,
himself one of the victims of a bomb attack.

The Attorney General had a dual role, said the Judge,
"He wears two hats. On the one hand he acts as the legal
adviser to the government. On the other, he has to ensure that
the rights of the individual are protected." In this case, the
Attorney General had been wearing his non-political hat. In
the light of all the evidence and the submissions, how did the
Crown's case stand? The Judge's answer was concise:

In no case does the Crown seek to establish that any of the individual accused have set off an explosive device or put an explosive device in the place where it was intended to explode. They don't have to establish that anyone did that act in order to convict for the offence of conspiracy. The Crown say that you cannot accept as even reasonably possible the massive dishonesty that would be involved in planting, involving so many police officers from high to low rank, involving such significant coincidences in what was planted at the flat and what was found there otherwise. They say you cannot accept that police perjured themselves to such a degree to cover the wicked assault on Greenfield by three police officers. You cannot accept, they say, the gigantic perjury that would be involved if the allegations made by the defence were right.

He concluded:

Consider the case of each accused separately, even though in the case of the first four those cases substantially coincide. Consider each charge separately. Remember the Crown has to prove its case. The standard of proof is that which makes you satisfied, that you are sure that guilt has been proved according to the evidence. Don't let prejudice cloud your judgement. Think not of your task as the exercise of some power, think of it rather as exercising your right which this country gives you to arrive at guilt or innocence. Consider that as your right, using your knowledge of the world and your common sense, bringing it to bear on the evidence you have heard.

That evidence had filled the lives of the twelve jurymen for more than half a year. The judge himself had taken eight days to sum it all up with an estimated quarter of a million words. In a sense, his treatment of the case in his summing up underlined the total split between prosecution and defence. He gave roughly equal time to both.

Seldom has a jury been battered with so much information, so much emotion. No wonder that their deliberations were to take some time.

CONCLUSION

The jury compromise . . . Verdict and sentences . . .
Special Branch worries

AT THE END of any major trial, the huge waiting hall outside
the various Old Bailey courtrooms takes on something of the
atmosphere of a Riviera gambling casino—quiet, tense, with a
kind of subdued excitement; at the end of the Angry Brigade
hearings, even more so. Special Branch men chatted casually
to the reporters covering the trial, speculating on the verdicts,
betting on the length of the sentences. In the street outside, a
group of thirty or so from the Stoke Newington Eight Defence
Group who had done so much work round the trial preparing
transcripts, publishing articles, helping to trace witnesses, kept
up their vigil, marching with their banners round the public
convenience on the traffic island opposite the Judge's entrance.

The jury had retired to consider their verdicts just after one
o'clock on 4 December. Already, at one hundred and nine days,
the trial was the longest in the history of the Central Criminal
Court, and that looked like just the beginning of the records.
For the first time at the Old Bailey, the Chief Administrator, Mr
Leslie Boyd, made arrangements to swear-in four extra jury
bailiffs to live with and look after the twelve men while they
continued their deliberations at a "private and secret place".
Rooms were booked for the jury in a hotel nearby. Just after
five o'clock, amid great security, they were taken there in a
white minibus. The Judge let it be known that he would be
available to hear their verdicts from ten o'clock the following
morning.

The first flurry of activity came at around midday when the
jury sent out a written question to the Judge. They wanted him
to remind them if there was any evidence to say why the police
had not evacuated Amhurst Road after they had found the
explosives. Mr Justice James told them that the police had
stopped the search of the flat immediately explosives and
detonators had been found. They had called in an explosives
expert at once, who had told them that the gelignite was in good

condition. But the question had not been canvassed, and it had not been suggested in cross-examination that the police ought to have given that evidence. No one seemed to think that it was necessary to raise the issue.

The jury were apparently satisfied. There were no further questions. But already the Old Bailey "regulars" were talking knowingly about what must be going on in the jury room. Judging from the length of time they had been out, they were obviously in difficulties, struggling to reach a decision. Sure enough, after more than thirty hours, they came back in again to tell the Judge that they could not reach a unanimous verdict.

"Having regard to the passage of time," said Mr Justice James rather sadly, "I am prepared to accept a majority verdict."

The atmosphere grew even more tense now. The hours passed slowly until at around five o'clock in the evening, led by an obviously weary foreman still in his shirtsleeves, the jury took their places for the last time. They had found four of the accused—Barker, Greenfield, Mendelson and Creek—guilty on the main count, conspiring to cause explosions between January, 1968, and August, 1971. On that charge the majority was ten to two. Unanimously, the four others, Christie, Bott, Weir and McLean, were acquitted of all charges against them, and discharged. Greenfield and Mendelson were also acquitted of two charges of attempting to cause explosions at Paddington police station and the Italian Consulate in Manchester. But they, and Barker and Creek, were found guilty of the possession charges, so obviously the defence allegations, that the material at Amhurst Road had been planted, had failed. The jury chose to believe the police. But in the case of the detonators in Stuart Christie's car, they apparently did not. He was acquitted of all the possession charges as well as the main conspiracy count.

After he had delivered their verdicts, the foreman turned to the Judge: "Us members of the jury would like to ask your lordship for—I believe the word is leniency or clemency—but that is what us members of the jury would like to ask."

Mr Justice James said he would certainly take that into consideration, and then, addressing himself to the four left in the dock, he said:

The conspiracy of which you have been convicted had as its

object the intention of disrupting and attacking the demo-cratic society of this country. That was the way it was put by the Crown, and that is the way it has been proved to the satisfaction of the jury once the suggestions of planting of evidence had been got rid of on overwhelming evidence.

The philosophies which you subscribe to are those which are set out in the various Angry Brigade communiqués. This conspiracy was alleged to have extended from 1968 until August, 1971, but it is clear that the evidence was stronger against each of you in respect of the latter stages of that period than it was in respect of the earlier stages.

For the purposes of sentence, I propose to disregard any of the incidents which occurred before responsibility is claimed by the Angry Brigade communiqués. That shortens the period and reduces the number of explosions.

The means that you adopted could have been even more lethal than they were, but I am satisfied on the evidence that the devices you used were not deliberately designed to cause death or serious injury, but rather damage to property.

Nevertheless, in every one of these cases, there was a risk of death or serious injury. Fortunately, only one person suffered any injury. There is, however, evidence that it is fortunate that no one was killed.

Your participation arose because you objected to the orderly way of society. One of the most precious rights is that an individual should hold his own opinions and be able to express them and be able to protest, and when one finds others who set out to dominate by exercising their opinions to the extent of enforcing them with violence it undermines that precious right.

I am not going to lecture you. I am sorry to see such educated people in your situation. Undoubtedly a warped understanding of sociology has brought you to the state in which you are.

The jury have asked me to take a course which will show mercy. In such a case as this the sentence called for by these offences must be a substantial one, and there are limits to which a court can give effect to such a recommendation, but I will do it to the utmost that I think right.

I treat you all as persons of good character. You, Greenfield and Barker, have previous convictions, but in dealing with these matters antecedents and previous history can have little effect, save to explain the situations in which you are.

Undoubtedly you have in many of your interests sought to do good and have done good, and I count that in your favour. But when all is said and done the public is entitled to protection.

Everyone must know that anyone who seeks to behave in this manner, holding explosives and weapons, must expect severe punishment. I am going to reduce the totality of the sentences, by reason of the jury's recommendation, by five years.

So, largely because of the jury's strong plea, then, Barker, Greenfield, Mendelson and Creek were sentenced to ten years each instead of the fifteen-year stretch that Prescott had been given on the same conspiracy charge by Mr Justice Melford Stevenson. Concurrent with the ten-year sentences, each was given eight years for possessing explosives, three years for possessing two sub-machine guns, two years for possessing a Browning pistol, and two years for possessing eighty-one rounds of ammunition.

There was no sign of emotion from the four as sentences were passed, the only comment came from Anna Mendelson as she left the dock. She said, "I would like to say thank you to the two members of the jury who had faith in us." It was a sentiment reiterated by Barker and Creek too, as they left the courtroom. In fact, their decision to trust in and try for a working class jury had obviously been the right one. Because of the way they saw the case, in class terms, two members of the jury had decided early on that they were not going to convict any of the eight at any price. Three others were inclined to be sympathetic to the defendants. Seven were prepared to convict them all, on all charges. It was the foreman's task to reconcile their differences. For fifty-two hours he tried. In the end, to get a ten to two majority, the only way out of the impasse was a kind of deal or compromise with the three "waverers": four convictions in exchange for four acquittals, and a strong recommendation for mercy.

As if to anticipate the controversy over his original decision to allow such a specific selection of the jury, Mr Justice James, before the court was finally cleared, made a statement. He said the trial he had just heard was a "very special one on its own facts. The course I took ought not to be, and was not intended to be, taken as a precedent for other cases."

There were objections, he went on, to any general application of selecting juries in this way, because it limited the selection to a small cross-section of the public, deprived juries of the help and expert skill of those invited to stand, and interfered with the rights of citizens who had jury qualifications.

"I want to make it absolutely clear," he warned, "that I would find it difficult to contemplate another case in which I would have arrived at the same conclusion."

But as far as the police were concerned, it was too late. To Bond and Habershon and the dozens of police officers who had spent so long on the case, the result was obviously disappointing. They thought they had found the evidence to convict all the defendants; the jury disagreed. The "classic conspiracy", as Bond called it, was proved to be only partially true. But there were consolations. The case had been solved within the standards and resources of present day law enforcement, by rules that were there for all to see. The police felt their involvement was reasonable. At no time was there any need to resort to the kind of recommendations in Brigadier Kitson's book. The Brigadier believes that the armed forces should be brought into the business of combating subversion from the very beginning: "There is no danger of political repercussions to this course of action, because consultations can be carried out in strictest secrecy."

In fact, in the Angry Brigade case, there was scarcely any co-operation between the security services and the police. Quite the contrary: when the Home Office were offered the mountain of information Habershon and his men had gathered on the whole area of libertarian politics, they seemed less than interested.

But despite this, there is no question that the Special Branch at any rate are concerned generally about the possibilities of "outside" interference in their work, particularly from military intelligence. It is not entirely professional jealousy. The two groups have different accountabilities. It is the army's task to carry out orders approved by their political masters, the government of the day. The police on the other hand do not derive their authority from the government, central or local, but from the people through Parliament, whose laws they have the job of enforcing. Only Parliament can widen or restrict the power of the police, and this they feel is a safeguard the military lack.

The Angry Brigade, by the illegality of their actions, forced these issues into the open, and posed some awkward questions for the authorities. Just how far should their political activities be circumscribed, and who should bring those activities to a close? The Security Services, the old MI5 and related departments, grew up to counter threats to the country inspired from abroad, from foreigners. But the young libertarians who formed the Angry Brigade circle were certainly not backed by Moscow, or any other foreign power. They were strictly home-grown subversives, owing allegiance to no one but themselves. If they really are "a bacillus which can infect the whole nation", as one security chief put it, then the Special Branch, as an arm of the police force, and therefore more accountable to the people at large, feel *they* should be left to deal with the infection. The Kitsonians, on the other hand, are for a much wider anti-subversive organisation, of which the Special Branch would be just a part. The struggle between the two groups, or rather sets of *modi operandi*, is unlikely to be made public. But, however it resolves itself, whatever the outcome, the Angry Brigade, under any other name, prepared the ground, as one of those closest to the group explained:

I think the Angry Brigade was in a situation where it was trying to reach into the context of struggling illegally against the particular political class that exists at the moment. It was just trying to develop different forms of struggle which it thought were effective. They were the first people to have actually taken up this position. The significance of what they've done won't become clear for some years. I think in, say, three or four years' time, even longer, people will relate to what they've done now, and will think about it, and think it's important.